By Plane, By Bus, By Car, By Foot

Here and There

by

Ursula Bendix

Memoir Books
Chico, California

By Plane, By Bus, By Car, By Foot
Copyright ©2025 by Ursula Bendix

ISBN: 978-1-937748-41-8 paperback
ISBN: 978-1-937748-42-5 epub

Library of Congress Control Number: 2025905604
First Edition

Photos: Ursula Bendix

Front Cover: Village street, Colombia, 1969
Back Cover: Little boy in South America, 1969
Half-title page: Facatativá Central Plaza, 1969
About the Author page: Ursula Bendix in Facatativá

Memoir Books
An Imprint of Heidelberg Graphics
Chico, California 95926
HeidelbergGraphics@gmail.com

CONTENTS

PART II

It . . .
>*borders on the delusional,*
>>*Perhaps even madness,*
>*This relationship I have*
>>*With the cactus in my office.*

The day begins with a warm greeting,
>*"How did you pass the night?"*
And ends in the evening with,
>*"Stay well and goodnight."*

This verdure companion,
>*This silent friend,*
Is ever joyful and full of hope
>*That each day brings forth a new bud.*

Ursula Bendix

Part I

CHAPTER 1

FOR WHOM THE BELLS TOLL

The bells tolled at 6:00 every work-day morning. Then a raspy recording of "Ave Maria" blared across the village square, after which, with much clearing of his throat, the parish priest, also with a very raspy voice, using a loudspeaker, admonished residents who had not paid their co-operative dues or had somehow transgressed. He announced upcoming church and community events and ended his broadcast by reminding parents to get their children ready for school. Most mornings I would disregard this daily half-hour interruption to my sleep by putting a pillow over my head once the bells began to toll. But a certain conversation with Padre Manuel Fernando Hidalgo one afternoon changed my cavalier attitude toward this ritual.

During much of my stay in Colombia in the late 1960s, I lived in Sesquilé a small town northeast of Bogotá, the capital. While there, I rented a room from a Colombian family whose house was very close to the central plaza and to *La Inmaculada Concepción de Sesquilé*, the only church in town. I liked living in this picturesque mountain town located some 8,500 feet above sea level in the *altiplano* of the Eastern Range of the Andes. Although laid out in a similar fashion to neighboring Andean towns with small stucco buildings, faded blue or red or white exteriors surrounding the plaza, anchored at one end by a small, benign-looking church, Sesquilé's newly constructed church, with its twin bell towers, was an impressive and demanding structure giving the town a more serious quality.

The town was founded in 1600 by Spanish explorers in search of gold in Lake Guatavita. The lake, just a few miles north of Sesquilé, is the suspected site of the El Dorado legend. Legend has it that the chief of the Muisca Indians, an indigenous Colombian tribe now vanished, would cover himself in gold dust during a ceremony honoring the goddess Guatavita. He would then board a raft made of reeds that was rowed to the middle of the lake where he would jump into the water to wash off the heavy gold dust. Worshippers on shore, seeing that the chief had jumped into the lake, would then throw trinkets of gold and precious stones into the water. This Muisca tradition thus became the origin of the legend of *El Dorado* meaning "the golden one," or "the man covered with gold." Numerous attempts have been made to drain the lake in order to find the treasures thought to be deposited there—without success.

I especially liked living with the Peña family. They were very protective and kind to me, a 22-year-old American girl with little teaching experience presuming to advise Colombian elementary school teachers on modern pedagogy. I will be forever grateful to the Colombian teachers who took a philosophical attitude towards this pretension: *First, the*

French came to show us new and better teaching methods; now the Americans are here with television programs and modern math. What never changes are our salaries. No one in the family questioned my competency or reason for being in Colombia. They did, however, gently help me navigate local customs.

I was advised to dress similarly to Colombian female teachers. Dresses or skirts—no pants ever. To this I rigorously adhered. I even had several skirts and suit jackets sewn by local seamstresses for a more professional look. I put on jeans only when I was planning to stay home. Because the house was walled on all sides with a courtyard in the center, no one could see my attire when I decided to go casual. The family's teenage girls, who never wore pants even while doing household chores, thought that that was so American, but enjoyed my daring.

On one such occasion, I had finished a letter I wanted to mail before the post office closed. Dare I take a chance and cross the plaza wearing jeans? Surely wearing jeans on one occasion was not going cause some diplomatic breach in Colombian-American relations nor was it going to be the cause for all Peace Corps Volunteers to be expelled from Colombia. I hurried across the plaza, mailed the letter and hurried back when I heard someone call to me.

«*Señorita, ven acá, por favor.*"

I stopped and stood frozen in place with fear. *That familiar, raspy voice. Didn't it wake me every morning?* I looked toward the church. There he was at the top of the church steps, towering above me, wearing his long, black cassock, an imposing and menacing figure, waving for me to come. Historical accounts of the Spanish Inquisition came to mind as I willed myself to slowly walk up the steps to him.

«*Buenas tardes, Padre Hidalgo.*"

«*Perdóneme señorita. A mí me parece que las mujeres que llevan pantalones no se ven tan bien desde atrás.*"

«*Lo siento.*»

What could I say, but "I'm sorry." Sorry that I was wearing pants. Sorry that he doesn't think women look good in pants from behind.

«*Con permiso.*»

Like a wayward child I acknowledged my guilt with a slight curtsy, excused myself and practically ran down the steps and around the corner to the safety of the Peñas' house.

Señora Peña, who was sweeping the patio as I entered, looked at me with concern.

«*¿Qué pasa, señorita?*» She wondered if something had happened.

«*Nada, nada.*» I assured her and excused myself. «*Con permiso, señora.*»

My worry began. Each morning, for the next two weeks, I would sit up in bed when the bells began to toll and listen. Would I be included in the day's admonitions resounding throughout the plaza? Would the transgression of *la señorita del Cuerpo de Paz* become public knowledge? Would the bells that day toll for me?

It became a tiresome endeavor and I soon went back to my old habit of drowning out the 6:00 a.m. call to action with my pillow. To make sure there was no lingering or possible retribution, I asked Señor Peña, landlord and the family patriarch, if he had heard any unpleasant news about me from Padre Hidalgo. No, the padre was planning his trip to Rome and the Vatican and was very busy. He might not return to Sesquilé if *el Papa* granted him, miracle of miracles, a position at the Vatican.

«*Qué bueno. Espero que sí.*» "How nice. I hope so," I commented with relief.

And miracle of miracles, the bells of *La Inmaculada Concepción de Sesquilé* did not toll for me during my stay in Colombia.

CHAPTER 2

THE TREE OF CONTENTION

It is a beautiful sunny Sunday afternoon, 13 February 2022. The neighborhood is peaceful. I suspect most of the neighbors are watching Super Bowl LVI. Why Roman numerals are used to name this year's contest is a mystery to me. Perhaps this has always been done, but I find it to be a peculiar nomenclature for such a distinctive American sport. How many of us would have known what the L stands for had we not heard a sports announcer mention it to describe this year's gladiator event. The naming of the contest between football rivals is of no real consequence when a possible war between the Western and Eastern powers, we are warned, is imminent. I suspect, however, that the outcome of Super Bowl LVI and the spectacle of the half-time show are of greater interest to most of my neighbors.

I too, in spite of grave danger and loss looming on the horizon, am focusing on a concern closer to home: my front lawn. The local weekly newspaper gardening expert advised getting lawns ready for the spring and summer growing seasons. This would require thatching, aerating, and fertilizing.

Using my antique metal rake, I begin the difficult thatching of grass, which has been plastered down by an unusually lingering snow pack. The rake and the grass are in a tussle as I pull this way and that way, but soon there are small piles of dry grass ready to be collected into a large plastic bag.

While collecting the thatched grass, I think of the little flowering tree that had occupied a very tiny space on my front lawn. Reluctantly, I had cut it down the year before, after most of its leaves had fallen. It seemed to become smaller each year—fewer branches produced flowers in the spring and the trunk was splitting. I had given it twelve years of care, fertilizing and watering it in hopes that it would find the strength to grow, but it languished, never becoming the magnificent flowering tree I had imagined it would be. A small handsaw was sufficient to sever its trunk. A tiny white worm had crawled out of the stump. There then was the culprit that had victimized my little tree.

Scooping up more dry grass, I think of another well-cared-for-tree that I hope has had a kinder fate.

I rented a room in the home of a wonderful Colombian family while working in the Peace Corps more than fifty years ago. Their house, situated on a corner lot close to the main plaza, was walled in on all sides with a patio in the middle, similar to many houses throughout South America. The Peñas, a little more prosperous than their neighbors, owned an additional adjoining lot, also walled in. A garden door, from the patio, made access to the *jardín*, the garden, easy.

In the middle of the garden stood the one and only tree growing in the neighborhood. On the rare, truly warm and sunny day, I would take a book to read and sit under the tree. When the daytime temperature reached seventy degrees Fahrenheit and I needed to wash my hair, I would ask for warm water to be heated in my wash basin on the kitchen wood-burning stove. I would take the warm water to the garden, and using the water judiciously, wash my hair kneeling under the tree. Señor Peña made sure I had privacy and did not let anyone enter the garden until I finished and was back in my room.

I remember the tree fondly. No one knew what species it was, but we all admired the dark green leaves and the straight branches reaching for the sky. Because of its location, high in the Andes and close to the equator, it never shed its leaves. Its crown was always full and stately.

The tree was much admired. It was taken care of with scrupulous punctuality. Every Monday morning Señora Peña would enter the garden with a bucket of water and slowly walk around the base of the tree pouring out the water. In the evening Señor Peña would accuse her of wasting water because the tree, obviously, didn't take in water from the ground, but through its leaves. *Why else would God send us rain?*

She had tried to convince him that the rain seeped into the ground allowing the tree's roots to tap into the water. No matter. On Tuesday, he would connect the water hose to the well and spray water as far up as a he could into the branches.

One evening when the discussion became somewhat heated between Señor Peña and the Señora, they asked me to tell them who was right. What a predicament. I liked them both and wasn't sure how to respond. I ended up explaining that it had become customary to mist plants in the States and also to water plants at the base. In fact, many households had misters, little plastic bottles that could spray water on the leaves of the plant. To insure further growth of plants, plant owners would also pour water near the base of the plant. In fact, I pointed out, their method of watering was very advanced and modern.

During my stay with the Peñas, Monday morning watering continued and so did Tuesday misting. The tree looked strong and sturdy when I left. Should I ever travel to Colombia again, I would certainly visit Sesquilé to greet the wonderful Peña family and check on their lovely tree.

———

I am finished thatching the lawn. Will it still be here, fifty years later to adorn the little cottage on a historic street in a small Northern California town?

CHAPTER 3

BUS TRIPS

Buses have been an integral part of my travels. I remember my first bus trips from Pfungstadt, Germany, to Darmstadt, in the state of Hesse, as an eight-year-old with my very best friend Christine who was three years older. Her father, a dentist, would send her to Darmstadt to pick up some needed supplies for his practice. She would ask me to come along on the short bus ride. The ride was perhaps less than thirty minutes, but an adventure for us—just the two of us, no adults. We would get off in the center of Darmstadt, the *Marktplatz*, and then walk to whatever store was on her father's list.

This was the early 1950s. We passed huge piles of rubble everywhere—remnants of the destruction caused by WWII bombings of the city. I don't remember being afraid. I also can't remember being told by our parents to watch out for unsavory individuals who might harm us. If we got lost, we should ask an adult for directions and be home for dinner.

I loved these bus trips with Christine. We had been given tasks, and we were trusted to be capable to perform them.

A few years later, my family emigrated from Germany to the United States. Now in Oregon, an element of fear was introduced to all activities. As high school students, girlfriends and I would take the TriMet buses to downtown Portland and spend Saturday afternoons perusing the large department stores. Their parents were somewhat reluctant to give them this freedom, setting precise timetables, and putting warnings and restrictions on these innocent outings. I chafed at these rules and would sometimes set out alone for the center of town. I enjoyed walking along the Park Blocks, that long, tree-lined median in the center of Portland, when the weather was nice and sitting on the steps of the Portland Art Museum pretending I was taking a break from an art class. (Some years later, my pretense became a reality.)

Art, especially Mexican art, was a passion of mine. Diego Rivera and José Clemente Orozco, two of Mexico's great muralists, were my favorites. In the summer of 1965, at the age of twenty, I set off with a university classmate on a Greyhound bus to Guadalajara, Mexico, to take a summer course: "Mexico, A History in Art." The bus trip took fifty-six hours and covered 3,672 km, approximately 2,282 miles.

When we changed buses at Nogales, Arizona (ready to cross the Mexican border), Janice and I shook hands with a smile—this was it. Led by smartly uniformed drivers, a new cast of travelers was accompanying us now on our grand adventure.

There were innumerable stops along the way to our destination—the Guadalajara bus terminal. At each stop, local vendors met our bus with their wares. I can still smell the wonderful aroma of the tortillas and *pan dulces* they offered for sale. But, being the cautious *gringas* we still were, we limited ourselves to Fanta, a familiar bottled soft drink, and packaged cookies—missing out on the culinary delight of the Mexican home-made tortilla.

Hungry and somewhat disoriented, we arrived in Guadalajara three days after leaving Portland, Oregon. Our Mexican host family, after greeting us at the bus station, asked if we were planning to travel back to the United States by bus. Did we look so travel-worn? We assured them that the bus trip home would be much easier now that we understood how to prepare ourselves for the journey.

The discomfort of our Portland-to-Guadalajara trip did not discourage us from exploring Mexico. In fact, we became very familiar with the central bus station in Guadalajara. As there were no summer classes on Fridays, Janice and I would set out early in the morning for the bus station, and purchase our tickets for coastal destinations such as Puerto Vallarta, Manzanillo, Zihuatanejo, Mazatlán, and Acapulco, or Lake Chapala, much closer to Guadalajara. Puerto Vallarta had a special fascination—the actors Elizabeth Taylor and Richard Burton had purchased houses there while filming "Night of the Iguana" in 1962, only three years prior to our stay in Mexico.

This couple held a romantic fascination in our young hearts. On each visit to Puerto Vallarta, we would pass by their homes (they owned separate houses connected by an overpass). We hoped to catch a glimpse of them walking across the little bridge hand in hand. What could be more fabulous than the tropical love affair of two exotic film stars?

Our bus trip home to Portland was uneventful—we slept most of the way. When awakened at the various bus stops, we indulged, without hesitation, on the *burritos* and *pan dulces* offered for sale by the vendors greeting new arrivals. I have been fortunate that in all of my travels I have never been subject to any of the intestinal maladies that seem to afflict other travelers.

It would be two years before I again enjoyed the adventures of bus travel—this time as a Peace Corps Volunteer in Colombia, South America.

I spent more than two years traveling by bus to the various villages in the Department of Cundinamarca visiting local elementary schools giving workshops and participating in curriculum discussions. When buses were not available, I walked or thumbed my way from one village to the next.

Mandatory monthly Peace Corps Volunteer meetings were always held in Bogotá. How did most of us travel there? By bus, of course. I shall always remember *Calle Cartoce*. Buses would pull up at the various stops—the bus driver's assistant hanging out of the front door shouting out the bus's destination—no need to know how to read.

One of the Volunteers was stationed in Facatativá a small town northwest of Bogotá. Those of us waiting for our bus hoped that his would arrive first so that we could see his discomfort when, from the approaching bus, the bus assistant shouted out, *« ¡Faca, Faca, Faca!"* One of the Volunteers, pretending he didn't understand Spanish, would nudge him and quietly say, "Hey John, is the bus going to f*** ya, f*** ya, f*** ya?"

Colombia seems synonymous with bus rides. Of the hundreds, maybe thousands, of miles I traveled by bus during my two-year tenure in Colombia, some trips are more memorable than others.

My job as an Educational Television Volunteer was to travel to various small country schools and hold workshops for elementary school teachers in techniques to incorporate into their daily lesson plan the fifteen-minute academic television programs that had been developed for grades one through five by Colombian master teachers and the Peace Corps at the Bogotá television studio. Monies from both the U.S. Agency for International Development and the Colombian government helped to place one thousand television sets in schools throughout Colombia. This was, at that time, the largest educational television system in the world. I was assigned schools located in the Department of Cundinamarca in the Andes. Most of these schools were in villages whose altitude was well over 8,000 feet above sea level. Travel to the schools was frequently problematic: bus schedules were irregular or non-existent. I often walked miles or hitched rides from one village to the next.

Bus rides in the Andes were not for the fainthearted. Many of the roads were narrow and unpaved. Every driver, rounding a blind bend in the road, blasted his horn, crossed himself, stepped on the gas, and put his fate as well as the fate of any passengers in God's hands. Motor fatalities along the roads were numerous. Memorials of crosses decorated with pictures of the Virgin Mary or Christ—with an exposed bleeding heart and bouquets of artificial flowers—dotted the roadsides. The spectacular scenery, the near head-on collisions, and the feeling of being airborne when looking down the mountainside, however, made each journey an adventure. Night trips, although more precarious, had their own appeal: lights from homes scattered over the dark, tall mountains always gave me the feeling of being among the stars in the sky.

During the first Christmas in country, a friend in a neighboring Department invited me to visit. This required a rather long bus journey, but it was an opportunity to see more of Colombia. It had rained continuously for several days. The mountains were cloud-covered and misty, the roads muddy streams. This did not deter me or the Colombians who boarded the bus at each roadside stop. I noticed that the passengers crossed themselves as they entered the bus. My religious beliefs are somewhat vague, but it occurred to me it might not be a bad idea.

As nothing alarming had occurred, my confidence in the bus driver increased and I fell asleep. I'm not sure how long I was asleep when I felt the bus sliding around a corner and heard the driver scream, « *¡Silencio!*" The bus came to a sudden stop having collided with an enormous mudslide. From my window seat, I saw how close to the edge of the cliff the bus had slid. Panic and fear gripped me. What if the bus continued to slide before I was able to exit? Was I supposed to die so young?

The driver commanded us to leave the bus slowly in single file. The passengers with small children, chickens, and rabbits took, what seemed to me, an inordinate amount of time getting off. I could not move, as I was hemmed in at the rear of the bus. I wanted to yell, "Just take the children and leave the animals behind." My Spanish failed me. As I watched the others' slow departure, I became convinced that the chickens and rabbits would live, and I would be hurled, still inside the bus, down the mountainside.

Once off the bus, I tried to maneuver carefully through the mud and debris. One of my shoes was pulled off in the process. When I bent down to retrieve it, two men came up behind me. I didn't remember either of them being on the bus. They were taller and sturdier than the average Colombian male, their faces serene and angelic. One lifted me up and carried me across the slide. He set me down on a rock near a rapidly running stream that had undoubtedly been one cause of the slide. His companion followed us with my muddy shoe in hand. I sat stunned and helpless as the man who had carried me took off my other shoe and began to wash my feet in the stream. He then dried them with his suit jacket. The other washed both my shoes with his handkerchief and used his coat as a towel. He placed the not-quite-dry shoes on my feet. Whereupon both men stood up, turned, and left. They never spoke to me. They did not board the replacement bus that came hours later. They disappeared.

I know that the bus accident happened, but I sometimes wonder if my memory of the angelic-looking men who helped me is real, or just a memory of a dream I had before being awakened by the collision. When I am not in a hurry and I let the story play out, I am grateful to have such a wonderful memory of their act of kindness.

Traveling by plane within Colombia was a luxury I could not afford. By a fortuitous event one afternoon in a Bogotá café, I was offered a free flight from Bogotá to Cartagena where a group of Peace Corps Volunteers would meet for a few days of fun in the sun. It was three days of enjoyment—a little romance, wonderful Colombian and Caribbean music, great food, relaxation in the sunshine on soft, white sand beaches, and touring *El Centro*, Cartagena's Old Town.

The weekend ended too soon. A long twenty-hour bus ride loomed ahead. I don't remember why we traveled in buses that rattled, without air-conditioning, through the tropical and semi-tropical landscape on our way to the 9,000-foot-high Andean capital, Bogotá. I suspect that money might have been the reason. Once we reached Medellín, at an elevation of 5,000 feet above sea level, we agreed it was time to stop for a couple of hours, and if need be, catch another bus later in the day.

We could not have chosen a more beautiful city—bougainvillea bushes bloomed everywhere, pink and purple blossoms decorated the city of eternal spring. The restaurant our taxi driver advised us to try was nestled on a hillside overlooking a coffee plantation. A waiter with practiced Colombian courtesy—showing no sign that our disheveled appearance did not merit the white cotton tablecloths, elegant dinnerware, and soft music being played—led us to a table near a huge window, which gave us an expansive view of the Aburrá Valley.

What was so poignant for me was not just the charm of the restaurant and its location, but the music. The music, so much of the ambiance for me, was the theme song from the movie "The Third Man." Anton Karas, who wrote the score, used the zither as the only instrument throughout. The film noir took place in Vienna after WWII—piles of rubbish everywhere, chaos, and the desperate conditions of its inhabitants. The music feels so happy, even though the film was a dark mystery. I watched the movie some years back. The music, then, as now, awoke happy memories of my childhood.

The rest of the trip home was long and arduous.

There were many more bus rides—in Peru, in Bolivia, in Ecuador, and in Chile—as I continued my travels through South America. They did not end, however, once I returned to the States.

My first full-time teaching job was at a Catholic boys' high school in Portland, Oregon. I was assigned the ski-team coaching position in addition to the six sections of assigned classes. During the ski season, the boys and I would board the ski bus for Mount Hood at 4:00 p.m. every Friday to take advantage of the reduced night skiing rates. I was the only adult assigned to the care and safety of the students. The bus driver was an employee of the bus company the school had hired, and he was out of commission during our time on the mountain.

Most of the trips were wonderful. A combination of events, however, led to one miserable Friday evening. After my fifteen- to twenty-minute lesson, the boys were able to ski freely on the mountain. I was making my way down a run when one of the senior boys stopped me to ask if he could return to the bus alone and stay there until we all left. Why? He had somehow managed to ski over one of his thumbs when he was crouching to make a jump. Should he have it examined at the first aid station? No, he was sure he had not broken it. He just wanted to sit out the rest of the evening. To this I agreed.

The weather began to change—in what seemed like minutes—as we headed down the mountain. The bus driver suggested we take the back-route home, which although longer, would most likely be safer in the whiteout conditions now present. As he slowly maneuvered the bus down the mountain road, a strange smell permeated the bus. The odor was almost unbearable. The treacherous conditions improved further down the mountain. As soon as he could, the driver stopped and walked to the back of the bus trying to determine what could possibly be causing the smell.

He had a disgusted look on his face when he approached me. One of the boys, the one with the wounded thumb, as it turned out, had vomited profusely all over himself, his seat, and a good portion of the back aisle. The driver insisted we stop at the nearest service station and hose out the entire bus as well as the perpetrator—and this was the last time he would drive a bunch of hooligans.

Hooligans?

Yes, hooligans! He had found an empty bottle of liquor in the back of the bus.

We arrived around midnight at the school, where an anxious group of parents awaited us. I explained the circumstances of our tardiness. I recommended to the parents, whose son's thumb was still causing him pain, to have the thumb checked the following day since the copious amount of alcohol he had consumed did not ease his pain.

Lesson learned! Always check the satchels of every student before letting him on the bus for Friday night skiing!

FLYING TO CARTAGENA

I must have missed the lecture on climate variation in Colombia during our Peace Corps training sessions at California State University in East Los Angeles. To be honest, the Colombian climate was not a priority for me, there was so much other information to learn: Spanish, the Colombian elementary school curriculum, Colombian customs and habits, the Colombian political system, and so on. I knew that Colombia is an equatorial country and assumed that meant the climate of the entire country to be warm or hot, never cold. Living in Los Angeles during June, July, and August might also have influenced my thinking. Every day was hot and Spanish was spoken everywhere. To someone from the cloudy, rainy Pacific Northwest this was similar to being in a foreign country—a warm Latin country.

I packed my green, Peace Corps-issued trunk accordingly—summer this and summer that, and just for good measure a couple of cardigans. The adventure beckoned and I was ready to meet the challenge.

During our orientation week in Bogotá, the capital, when our individual country location was assigned, I learned that Colombia has five climate zones: tropical rainforest, tropical savanna, tropical steppe, a desert zone and a mountain zone. My placement was in the mountain zone. Perfect. Living in the Andes had a dramatic and exciting appeal. What I didn't know was that elevation determines the climate in the mountain zone. Up to 3,000 feet above sea level was considered *tierra caliente* or the hot land; *tierra templada*, the temperate land, is found up to about 5,000 feet; up to 10,000 feet above sea level is *tierra fría*, the cold land; and land above 11,500 feet is considered *tierra helada*, the frozen land. Nothing much happens in the frozen land, we were told, no towns or trees are found there. I was fortunate to be placed down the mountain a bit into the cold land, where the sun rarely shines much from June to September, and it rarely gets above sixty degrees Fahrenheit during the day. The night temperature varies from cold to colder.

I was sure all would be fine once I secured warm living accommodations. I could always buy a jacket or coat. My mountain adventure began when I was dropped off by the area Peace Corps Representative in front of a private home in my assigned village, Sesquilé. Some negotiating was done for their extra room, but no meals. I was to eat my meals in the restaurant with other teachers not residing in town. The room was large with nicely polished wood floors, white, freshly painted stucco walls, a small wardrobe, and one dresser. Double doors opened directly to the tiled courtyard. I felt very fortunate.

Days were filled with meeting teachers, and school and town officials. My cardigans proved adequate. Evenings I was invited to join the Peñas and their seven children in the kitchen where the wood-burning stove warmed everyone before going to bed. I dreaded the end of the evening and the return to my ice box of a room. A space heater might have solved the problem, but it wasn't part of the negotiated rental agreement. Maybe there wasn't even such a thing in Colombia. My assignment was to help teachers incorporate 15-minute educational television programs into their curriculum, not to revolutionize their home heating system. I steeled myself. I simply needed to adapt.

My travel iron came to the rescue. I would plug the iron in before going to the evening warm-up in the kitchen. When I returned to my room, I would pull the blankets back from the bed, iron the sheets, unplug the iron and place it at the foot of the bed between the sheets, crawl into bed, and undress under the blankets that I had quickly pulled over the sheets again to conserve the warmth.

I did suffer a few burns when I forgot where I had placed the hot iron.

The first months passed quickly; there was so much do and learn. I bought a *ruana*, the Colombian version of a poncho, to stay moderately comfortable once the sun set. But adaption to the cold land wasn't happening quickly enough.

In my nightly dreams I am roasting a naked, plucked chicken over an open spit on a whitewashed beach. As I am turning the chicken, the tropical sun is burning my arms and back. Soon there is no difference between the chicken and me—we are both charred. Here the dream ends. Never mind the new burn on my leg. I was convinced my subconscious was at work.

A group of us living in the cold land decided what we needed was a brief vacation to *la tierra caliente* or better yet to tropical Cartagena, jewel of Colombia's Caribbean cities, home of the *cumbia* and *salsa*. Daytime on sunbaked beaches, evenings in nightclubs dancing to exotic sounds and drinking *Cuba libres* became a constant topic of discussion whenever we met.

How to get there? Would a few days of fun in the sun be worth a forty-plus-hour round-trip bus ride on torturous, meandering, and treacherous mountain roads? Flying, the preferred method of travel, even for Colombians, had its own drawback. First was the cost—on $79.00 a month Peace Corps pay, the expense of a ticket was enormous. Second, flying, within Colombia, had become more complicated since Bolivian soldiers—trained, equipped, and led by U.S. Green Berets and CIA operatives had assassinated Ernesto "Che" Guevara, the Cuban revolutionary, in the jungles of Bolivia not long after our group's entry in country. Baggage and documents of travelers were thoroughly checked by Colombian police and soldiers at every airport. Anyone looking in the least bit like a revolutionary or a Marxist was detained and questioned. American passports were no guarantee of safe travel.

Sitting in a café in Bogotá one afternoon with fellow Volunteers drinking *tintos*, small cups of black coffee sweetened with *panela* (raw sugar), the topic of Cartagena and how to get there soon pushed out our usual passionate discussions about Colombian educational shortcomings and political hypocrisies around the world. There was no way around it. If we really wanted to go, we would have to endure the dreaded bus ride.

We were totally engrossed in how and when to attempt the journey and didn't notice the man at the next table listening to us until he ventured, "I'm flying to Cartagena next week. Anyone want to come with me?"

Someone in the group replied, "What do you mean 'come with me'?"

Cindy, my closest friend in the group, moved a little nearer to me and whispered, "Do you think he's an American?"

I whispered back, "Look at his feet, they're huge. You know American men have the biggest feet on the planet. That's what Colombians say at any rate."

Not totally satisfied, Cindy tried the more direct route. "Who are you? You look and sound American, but are you some kind of undercover agent from the CIA?"

(One of our group's fears, even during training in L.A., was that a CIA agent was planted in the training group who would be able to enter Colombia with us for some nefarious U.S. government intelligence work.)

"Heck no. I'm Tom. I'm in the army, just a soldier, stationed here to watch for Russian satellites passing overhead."

Cindy, as always the most candid, asked, "You mean the U.S. Army?"

"Yeah, bet you guys didn't know we're here. We don't wear our army gear. Don't want to attract too much local attention."

Cautious Eric wanted to know, "Why are you spying on Russian satellites here? Can't that be done somewhere in the States? Are you inviting us to fly in an army plane to Cartagena?"

"Can't do that. I'm taking private lessons at the El Dorado airport here. I'm scheduled for more flying time next week. My instructor thought we might fly from Bogotá to Cartagena. It's only an hour and a half, one way. I could take one of you. Anyone interested?"

Silence.

Only one of us could go; the rest would have to take the bus. Was this a safe thing to do? But ninety minutes one way versus twenty plus hours—how would we decide who gets to fly?

And, who is this guy really?

Only Cindy and I were willing to take him up on the offer. The others were reluctant to chance a ride in a small private plane with a student pilot over the Andes.

She and I decided to draw straws. Whoever drew the long one would go with Tom. Eric selected two wood matches, broke them and arranged them in his hand.

I won the draw—but doubt set in. Did I win or lose?

Cindy and two or three other Volunteers would start out on Friday the following week and I would meet Tom at 11:00 a.m. on Saturday that same week at the Bogotá airport.

To what had I committed? Was Tom really a U.S. military man and not a smuggler of some sort using me as a decoy or a Marxist sympathizer trying to escape Bolivian, Colombian, and U.S. intelligence forces? To tell the truth, I didn't care. I just wanted to get to Cartagena to feel warm inside and out.

My doubts vanished when I met Tom and his instructor, Enrique, at the airport as planned. Enrique was a very handsome, pleasant, and cordial Colombian man, the very image of the dashing pilot from movies I had seen, wearing aviator glasses and a leather bomber jacket. He greeted me graciously with a slight bow and a handshake.

«*Muy buenos días, señorita. Usted es muy valiente.*"

Was I brave, as he suggested, or just foolish?

Tom and Enrique in front and I in the back, we were ready to take off. I braced myself as the plane moved faster and faster down the runway. The cows in the adjacent field ahead seemed to be getting closer. What separated us were a couple of barbed wires. Ever faster. But shouldn't the plane be leaving the ground by now? Yes, of course!

«*¡Tire hacia arriba!*" Enrique's not-so-calm voice instructed Tom to pull up.

From my view in back, I was sure we would collide with a cow or pull the fence up with us. Neither happened. The plane became airborne. Enrique turned around and gave me a thumbs up.

The Andes looked lovely from above in the bright sunshine and brilliant blue sky, snow and ice fields on the higher peaks. The sun warmed the cabin of the plane. I hadn't felt so warm in quite some time. My spirit soared. The hum of the plane's motor, the warmth of the cabin, and the occasional conversation between Tom and Enrique relaxed me—I fell asleep.

"Hey you. We're here." Tom tapped me on the shoulder.

Yes. I could smell and feel the tropical air of Cartagena as I climbed out of the plane.

"Tom, Enrique, *muchísimas gracias.*"

«*Señorita, usted debe tener buena conciencia—durmió durante casi todo el viaje.*"

Enrique thought I must have had an untroubled conscience since I slept most of way. I think it was much simpler than that—I was finally warm again.

We shook hands. They headed for coffee in the terminal, and I went to find a taxi that would take me to the hostel where the other cold land Volunteers and I were to meet.

CHAPTER 5

FROM CHILE, REGRETFULLY

20 April 2018

Dear Claire,

I have been in Chile a little over three weeks now. This is still autumn time in the southern hemisphere and the days are warm and sunny for the most part. There have been huge downpours occasionally—and all shiver, put on their heaviest coats, and lament the coming of winter. A prophecy of doom, the coming of the darkness prevails. I'm not sure if the fiction writers' stories of Armageddon are so far off the mark. Destruction hangs in the air, and fear reigns. I am apprehensive. What if I cannot tolerate being locked into a cold cement block house without central heat for days on end while the winds whirl around and the rain assails? Even the few days of rain I have experienced have frightened me. The streets fill with water that has nowhere to go. Rivers form, but there are no bridges to cross. Ironically, I live in a house on *Calle Río Bravo*—Fierce River Street.

To complicate the disparate feelings of the coming winter, an occasional tremor and movement from below adds to the tension and fear of the horror awaiting the populace. The 2010 earthquake whose 8.8 magnitude caused extensive damage to the Biobío Province has not been forgotten. Is it any wonder then that the only comfort available to the majority of the people is to eat and eat and eat some more? In fact, obesity has become a national disease according to the President of the Republic of Chile, Sebastian Piñera. The government has stepped in and now requires food producers to label containers with the caloric value per serving. Also, charming cartoon characters on cereal packages are no longer allowed to entice children. Time will tell if this will help the astonishing health problem facing this long, narrow Andean country.

I need to stop this dark rumination or I will want to escape. I signed a contract to teach English for four months and only a little less than a month has gone by. The high school I have been assigned has both technical training programs and a liberal arts component. Most of the students have to take some English classes. I think it is safe to say that ninety percent of the technical students don't care about learning English and perhaps (I am being generous) sixty percent of the liberal arts students don't care either.

I was informed yesterday that the teachers will go on strike on Thursday. Today that was confirmed—no school on Thursday. I can sleep in and then take the bus to Los Angeles, the capital of the Biobío province, look around a bit, and buy some supplies I need. If the strike lasts until Friday, I can travel a little further afield before winter really sets in. No such luck most likely.

21 April 2018

The teachers did strike on Thursday. I don't know what their grievances were—I never asked. I have no desire to get involved in school politics.

I had planned to take the bus to Los Angeles, the capital of this province, the day of the strike, but since I had seen the downtown and mall before, I decided to go with Gladys, my landlady, to the *feria*, the one-day-a-week market and take a look around. She quickly bought the week's essential produce for the household. She then hurried back to the house so that she could get ready for her doctor's appointment. I took advantage of the rest of the afternoon to do some banking and walk back to the *feria* to inspect more closely what the vendors were selling.

When I returned to the house, Gladys was already there. She invited me to join her and her sister at the weekly exercise class at the neighborhood recreation center. The exercise class consisted of about twenty-five men and women past sixty following some mental activities for cognitive development. The therapist mentioned that reading just fifteen minutes a day would keep the mind sharp. The physical therapist then led everyone in some simple stretching and balance exercises.

I looked over the next day's lesson plan (just in case the strike wasn't extended to Friday or beyond), took a nap before dinner, ate my evening meal with the two ladies, watched a little television news, and then went to bed. Altogether a very relaxing day!

All good things must come to an end. It was a one-day strike.

Before classes started this morning, I talked to Nadia Ramos, the head English teacher about the incessant demonstration of affection among the students. They are constantly touching and hanging on to each other. Teachers allow students to kiss them on the cheek when greeting or leave-taking. She said that the teachers discourage that behavior, but so far no luck. I try to anticipate this familiarity and extend my hand.

Andrés Ortiz invited me to *onces*, his family's evening meal. He will pick me up at 6:30 p.m. He told me both his son and daughter live in the States. His son works as the Chief Financial Officer for a huge Chilean lumber manufacturing company that is operating there. He, the son, is married to a Canadian national. His daughter is married to a U.S. citizen. They all see each other every six months when one or the other travels to the other's residence. The world has truly become small. Yes?

I am somewhat anxious about this dinner invitation. I want to be a gracious guest. I try not to refuse too many items I am served. It is my opinion, however, that Chilean food leaves much to be desired: little variation, bland, and fried. The ships carrying spices coming from the Orient passing through the Straits of Magellan hoping to connect to the Pacific Ocean, and Chile's coast must have succumbed to the treacherous sea. The constant loss of their cargos had an unfortunate effect on the Chilean cuisine.

I have a total aversion to the *yerba maté* tea so prevalent in Chile and Argentina. The *maté* tea is brewed from leaves of a small South American tree. It contains stimulants such as caffeine and theobromine which is also a stimulant that comes from the cacao beans. The tea tastes bitter and no amount of sugar seems to change that. It is definitely an acquired taste.

Surely the Ortiz family having traveled often to the States will take my American sensibilities about food into account. I hope they don't think I should experience a typical Chilean meal.

At the moment, I am contemplating not traveling around Chile after my teaching contract is finished. I might just fly directly back to California. Dreary winter landscapes aside, my anticipation of seeing gorgeous countrysides and eating fabulous exotic foods, has been squashed. This was supposed to be a life-enhancing experience. Crazy, yes?

In hindsight, viewing the remains of a crumpled Roman town somewhere in Italy might have been sufficiently fulfilling.

From Chile, regretfully . . .

CHAPTER 6

ON BEING A LODGER

I remember sitting in a window-seat of a *turbus* in the twilight hours of a Sunday afternoon as I was returning from Puerto Montt, one of the southernmost ports in Chile, watching the winter landscape float by—barren grapevines and naked fruit trees. I recall how my body tensed with each recognized landmark. The inevitable end to my escape loomed ahead.

I was returning to the home owned by the middle-aged widow Señora Gladys Salvado. I was the most recent in a series of lodgers to occupy her spare bedroom and have exclusive use of the second bathroom. Sometimes family members forgot this was "my" bathroom and intruded. Although I was not unreasonably offended when this happened, I decided not to leave my towel or soaps there. After each bathroom visit, I would take all items back to my room. This, of course, required me to remember to bring them with me again each time I used the bathroom. I thought about having a small towel and soap in the bath for daily use, but I was afraid that they would think that I did this for the family's convenience. All things considered, this was a small inconvenience for the luxury of having my own bathroom.

As I preferred not to have the landlady or her visiting children and grandchildren enter my room when I was not there, I made my own bed, changed the sheets, and swept the floor once a week, and always locked the door when I left. Unfortunately, I didn't discover that the key to my bedroom was also the key to the front door until a few weeks before my departure from Chile.

Again, all things considered, this living arrangement would have been fine had it not been for Señora Gladys Salvado's elderly sister who occupied the third bedroom at the far end of the house. I'm not sure who disliked whom first, but I think she had an aversion to me the minute we met. My hostility toward her grew, culminating in outright dislike. Mealtimes were the most difficult for me. She would watch me eat, telling Señora Gladys, before I even had a chance to finish the meal, what the cats would receive off my plate. I didn't care that the cats were given the portions I didn't eat; I just disliked her predicting from the beginning of my meal the cats' next meal.

Fortunately, we, the Señora Gladys, Señora Ruth, the sister, and I only ate our evening meal together during the work week. I had breakfast alone and rarely came to the house for lunch. I found that limiting my communal meal times was essential to maintaining a cordial relationship with the household. Leaving Friday afternoons to take sightseeing trips—and not reappearing until late Sunday evening—was, in my view, also necessary to preserving harmony with the ladies.

The weekend excursions to the southern coast of Chile, most specifically to Puerto Montt or into the foothills of the Andes were necessary not only for me emotionally, but also for my physical well-being. The damp and cold buildings of the local polytechnic high school in which I taught English and the mold in Señora Gladys' house had been making me physically ill.

I would travel the seven hours north by bus to Santiago, rent a room in a four-star hotel and relax; I could sleep as late as I wanted and, most importantly, eat what I wanted without scrutiny. The joy of walking alone along the cobblestone streets of the colonial sections of Santiago while imagining the life of its citizens in centuries past made the weeks ahead bearable. Ambling along the streets near the Plaza de Armas, scenes from *Inés del Alma Mía* (*Inés of My Soul*, Isabel Allende's historical novel of the founding of Chile's capital) became real. My difficulties paled when compared to the hardships encountered by the Spanish *conquistadores*. I had not come to find gold, and unlike those adventurers hundreds of years ago, I was not in search of something as grand as a new world—only golden experiences and one final adventure before settling into old age.

Chile, the southernmost country in the world and closest to Antarctica—with the scenic wonders of Patagonia, the Atacama Desert, the towering Andes, and its spectacular Pacific Ocean ports—had been my chosen destination. I was subsidizing this adventure by teaching English to Chilean high school students in schools that participated in the "English Opens Doors" program sponsored by the United Nations and Chile's Ministry of Education.

Since I had traveled much of northern Chile some fifty-plus years prior, I chose to be placed in a town in southern Chile, preferably in a coastal town south of Concepción, the second-largest city in Chile. My placement was in southern Chile all right, south of Concepción, but not on the coast. I was placed in a medium-sized town in Chile's agricultural and timber-growing area that resembled, ironically, my hometown in Northern California—where the end of the timber industry had brought poverty and unemployment to the region. Here also, with the closing of the largest radiata pine sawmill that had employed hundreds of workers, the town had a desperate and poor appearance. For the Chilean government, the thinking was that if the young people became proficient in English, their chances for employment would be improved when applying for work with U.S., Canadian, British, or Australian businesses in Chile. English would open doors.

My weekend escapes were most often in Puerto Montt. There I had found a luxurious hotel, close to the main plaza and Angelmo Harbor. I always asked for room 1001. I could keep the drapes open while lying in bed and enjoy a magnificent view of the Pacific Ocean. The room had floor-to-ceiling windows and sliding glass doors that brought in the most expansive view of the Pacific Ocean I had ever seen. The sea in the far distance formed a straight line with the horizon. It was easy to understand why ancient mariners believed that if sailing out toward the horizon, a ship was in danger of falling off the Earth.

My laptop was always connected and the television menu included programs from almost every corner of the world: news and movies in French, Portuguese, Mandarin, German, English were at my fingertips. There was also a wonderful German restaurant within walking distance of the hotel.

This southern part of Chile had been settled by Germans in 1853. The Chilean government had recruited thousands of German families to settle there with hopes that the settlers could quash the Mapuche Indians who were an obstruction to the development of the region. The German settlers coped with the Mapuches, built timber-framed houses similar to those in their homeland, and established Chile's dairy and cattle industry. German terms such as *kuchen* (cake), and *kartofel* (potato) became part of the local Spanish lexicon.

These words were not unfamiliar to me. Perhaps some of my German ancestors had ventured to this part of the world. My favorite dishes, prepared from the daily salmon catch at the Angelmo Harbor fish market became my preferred lunch and dinner choices at the Club Aleman restaurant.

When the longer seven-hour bus trips seemed too exhausting, I would take the bus to Concepción. Although there were a few stops along the way, I would arrive at the terminal in Concepción within an hour. From the terminal, I would walk to the *Universidad de Concepción*. The university has a wonderful art museum, museum store, and a tiny museum coffee shop. Before browsing the various exhibit rooms, I would visit the coffee shop and order one of their delicious desserts, coffee, or tea.

I had always secretly mocked acquaintances who, upon returning home from long and exotic travels, only talked about the restaurants or foods of the places they found along the way. I now understood how a satisfying a piece of cake, or a wonderful cup of coffee could color an experience. Satisfied and relaxed, I would study the huge mural painted by the Mexican muralist Jorge Gonzalez on the foyer walls before climbing the stairway to the galleries on the second floor. The mural was a gift from the Mexican government to the *Casa de Arte* after the 1960 earthquake had destroyed a large part of the university. The scenes depicting social upheaval, and the brutal elimination of Chile's native population rival those found on the walls of the *Palacio Nacional de México* painted by Diego Rivera.

Sometimes I would bypass the trip to the art museum and take a taxi to the south end of Concepción where I had located a very comfortable hotel, clean and warm. Close to the hotel was an Italian restaurant that offered the most delicious *gnocchi* smothered in an exquisite tomato sauce. Food and warmth had become a preoccupation of mine. Another benefit of the hotel was its residential location that allowed me to take very safe walks without fear of encountering a multitude of stray dogs, which always seemed to be roaming around the city center.

Thinking back now to this last bus ride from Puerto Montt along the Pan-American Highway to the small provincial Chilean town that had been my home for four months, I remember telling myself, as I remind myself now, that I had come as a volunteer to Chile in order to teach English to high school students. In exchange, my payment would be to participate in a different culture, to live with another family, to make acquaintances with young people from around the world, and to experience another encounter with the physical beauty of Chile.

This attempt to reassure myself, however, did not assuage my uneasiness as the bus pulled into the terminal. I stepped down slowly, waited for my suitcase to be pulled from the bowels of the bus, and adjusted my computer case and handbag in preparation for the mile-long walk to Señora Gladys' house—where I, for a short time longer, assumed my role as the family lodger before leaving Chile.

Profesora, my name is Matias and Lucy. We love much be careful, bye.

Profesora, la vamos a extrañar muchisimo usted es super simpática y muy buena Profesora es muy graciosa, etc. Cuidece muchisimo y espero verla luego muchos kises.

I love so much teacher.

Remember: Matias Quejada and Lucy Sepulveda 2B MC

28/06/2018

CHAPTER 7

MATIAS AND LUCY

This little handwritten note, surrounded by small, red hearts, with all of its imperfections is a most prized possession—a bitter-sweet reminder of the four months I spent in the Biobío Province of southern Chile teaching English to high school students at the Liceo Manuel Arístides Zuñartu Zuñartu, known in the region with its acronym as Liceo MAZZ.

I wanted one more adventure before settling down to old age. "Old age" by my definition begins at 80 years of age, which I was approaching quickly. I didn't want this to be just a travel vacation experience, one week in this or that country, two days in this or that city visiting famous museums, archeological sites, or treading carefully through architectural wonders. I have done this type of travel, but it always left me with a "that was okay" feeling. The many television travel documentaries I have seen have undoubtedly dulled my appreciation and curiosity about the many Wonders of the World.

When asked "How was the trip?" I, like other travelers I'm acquainted with, highlight and praise delicious and unusual meals eaten in small, out-of-the-way restaurants popular with locals, or the brief but personal encounters made with natives while stepping beyond guidebook recommendations. The traditional meals in these small establishments served by the owners or family members seemed more authentic, less touristy, often visually pleasing, sometimes producing a new tactile sensation; they nourished the body, and, paradoxically, the soul.

That is what I longed for, a soul-enriching experience.

Some complicated and fortuitous circumstances brought me in contact with a cadre of young people who travel the world teaching. University trained and proficient in English or Mandarin, these twenty-to-thirty-year olds come from countries such as the United States, England, Australia, New Zealand, China, Russia, and English-speaking Africa. They stay six months, a year, maybe two, in any country that has contracted with the United Nations for language teachers, and then move on. The host country provides for housing and a small stipend.

Although I was more than twice the maximum age limit advertised on the application form, my age (which I correctly stated) was never discussed, and I was accepted. Becoming part of this group that circled the globe was just what I wanted. I wouldn't be a tourist, but a temporary resident with a work permit and a host country bank account.

A half a century before, I had traveled by train and bus from La Paz, Bolivia to Santiago, Chile. My train ride over the Andes, stopping only at the frontier check point between Bolivia and Chile, at an altitude close to 14,000 feet, and then dropping down to the Chilean plateau skirting the Atacama Desert, with the hot wind blowing off the barren land through the open windows of my third-class train compartment, is one of my most remembered geographic travel experiences. Now I wanted to see southern Chile and be able to behold the beauty of Torres del Paine National Park in Patagonia and perhaps teach in a school in Punta Arenas at the tip of Chile, which would give me an opportunity to travel to the Chilean part of Antarctica.

On the application form, I mentioned my preference as southern Chile, preferably in a medium-sized town on the coast. I should have been more precise. Chile is a long, long, narrow country and southern Chile is twice as long as the entire length of California.

My placement was in a medium-sized town, as I had requested, in what is technically the southern region of Chile, but not as far south as I had had in mind—and I wasn't near the Pacific Ocean. My assignment was in the Biobío Province, one of the wine growing and agricultural areas of Chile between the coast range and the Andes, south of Concepción, the second-largest city in Chile. Isn't there a song by the Rolling Stones, "You Can't Always Get What You Want"? Looking out of the bus window as it pulled into the terminal of the city in which I was to teach and live for four months, I knew this to be absolutely true. This was not a coastal town—I had seen no evidence of the Pacific Ocean the entire three-hundred-mile bus trip from Santiago.

The principal of the school, a portion of the school band, a local newspaper reporter, and the two widowed señoras in whose house I would be lodged greeted me as I stepped off the bus. Maybe this was Providence's way of giving me that soul-enriching experience I thought I needed.

Liceo MAZZ is a polytechnic high school of almost 700 students in a town of approximately 20,000 that has fallen on hard times since the biggest employer, a very large radiata pine sawmill, closed a few years prior to my arrival. Ironically,

I had traveled 6,300 miles to arrive at a location similar to the one I left, a town in Northern California that has fallen on hard times since the loss of the timber industry. Perhaps my experience and understanding of radical economic change made me the most suitable to help these teenagers whose future looked somewhat tenuous.

English is a required subject for secondary students in Chile. Some of the schools begin their English education in fifth grade. I believe the thinking is that English will help the young people be better prepared for the modern world and perhaps obtain jobs in one of the many foreign companies that are so much a part of Chile's economy now that English is recognized as the business language of the world.

My understanding had been that I would act as a resource and aid for the four full-time English teachers. As it developed, I actually became the fifth English teacher. Each week I met with 440 students, in groupings of fifteen to twenty students, for forty-five minutes. I was asked to speak only English in the classroom, devise games, language drills, and in general try to improve the students' pronunciation and fluency in English—without reading or writing lessons—taking into account their grade level and their designation as either industrial arts students or liberal arts students. My after-school assigned activity was the debate team. I had to help prepare four seniors and an alternate to debate, in English, other regional *liceo* students on topics selected by someone in Chile's Ministry of Education. Liceo MAZZ hoped to win the regional debate, move on to the provincial debate and, hopefully secure a spot at the national high school student debate in Santiago.

I had absolutely no training or experience in the art of debate. I had never been on a debate team, never watched a high school debate team in action, and only understood that any given topic was to be either defended (the pro position), or argued against (the con position) by the members of a team. The stand the teams were to take was decided before the debate began. Winning such a contest was important to the members of the Liceo MAZZ team. It would give weight to a possible application and acceptance at a university upon graduation. My workload greatly exceeded my expectations; within a week, I was sure that my wish for a soul-enriching experience was not being denied. I trudged on.

During my twenty-plus years teaching in the U.S., I prided myself in learning all of my students' names within the first week of class, but 440 students—each with at least two first names and two last names—was more than my aged brain could recall. Matias and Lucy, however, distinguished themselves in a charming and somewhat peculiar way.

If my going-away note from Matias and Lucy seems more familiar in tone than any note a teacher might receive from high school students in the States, it didn't seem so to me by the end of the school semester. It was not uncommon for students, both male and female, who either had a female teacher for several years, or one they particularly liked, to greet the teacher by kissing her on both cheeks. Affection between students was also common. When I questioned the staff about this, they told me that although it was not condoned, they had a hard time stopping it. I, however, told my classes that touching, hand-holding, kissing, leaning on each other, and so on, was not allowed in my class and that I was too old to change my thinking on that subject. Most of the students accepted this restriction—in the classroom, at least.

Matias and Lucy were second-year industrial arts students. I never asked them their ages, afraid that they might ask me in turn, which if I answered, would somehow undermine my status and authority. On the young side of fifteen, they appeared to be friends, classmates—well-behaved and enthusiastic about learning English. Every teacher's ideal students.

I rarely ate my lunch in the faculty dining room. There was always so much to prepare for the next classes. Also, lunch being the principal meal in Chile, the faculty dining room became an aroma-filled chamber as teachers used the microwave or propane stove to heat their soups, casseroles, and meat dishes. I would bring a sandwich, a piece of fruit and drink with me to eat in the classroom. The landladies would heat their left-over lunch for me in the evenings for dinner.

Matias and Lucy, once they knew that I spent my lunch period in my classroom preparing for the next onslaught of students, would knock on my door, stick their heads in, tell me who they were, and if they could come in and talk with me. Of course they could, that was why I had been hired, to speak English with the students. They would move two chairs to the front of my desk, sometimes three if their friend Oscar accompanied them. Several minutes would pass during which they silently assessed what I was eating and what I was wearing—then the questions began: what did I think of the U.S. President (they did not like him); how much did my Calvin Klein jacket cost; was the Lenovo computer (the type I was using) better than an Apple computer; who was my favorite rapper, and so on. Not to disappoint them, I mentioned the only rapper's name I could remember, Snoop Dogg. How charmingly naïve, but at the same time complimentary—my age was not considered—they assumed we had the same interests.

How they knew about brands such as Nautica, Tommy Hilfiger, or Calvin Klein amazed me. I became aware of the internet's reach and influence in the world. Matias was interested in how much things cost and, without any hesitation, would ask me the price of the items he particularly liked. Maybe he was doing some comparison shopping between the States and Chile. Lucy never asked about my clothes; she was more interested in my family—where I lived, if I was married, how many children I had, and so on. After my initial hesitancy to answer questions of a personal nature, I accepted these lunch period conversations to be extraordinary. I did, however, tell them that I was not going to discuss either Chilean or U.S. politics.

When they ran out of questions, or if in some cases I told them a topic was private, Matias would sit across from me and stare at my eyes. He claimed to have never seen someone with blue eyes, and told me that my eyes were beautiful. He would spend most of my lunch period and theirs looking at my eyes. Lucy, who seemed uncomfortable with this turn in the conversation, would look at me apologetically and wait for the lunch bell. I don't think the color of my eyes was something she cared about, but she cared about Matias and tolerated his obsession with my blue eyes, only shrugging her shoulders when I would look in her direction, indicating how silly his prattle about blue eyes was. No American high school student would spend his lunch period looking at his teacher's blue eyes. I was uncomfortable at first, but after a time I accepted his fascination with my eyes and began to search for blue eyes among my Chilean acquaintances, staff, and students. There were none.

Perhaps I should have discouraged such personal attention, but soon I understood Matias's and Lucy's comments and questions for just what they were—interest in another culture and trying to acquire information and an understanding of me and my life in the States. If some remarks crossed the line—"*Profesora*, you have a nice figure," or "*Profesora*, I love you"—I made light of them. Language nuances translated do not always convey what was intended. I like to think that they just wanted to tell me that they liked having me there and did not quite have the language skills to communicate in a manner acceptable in most of the English-speaking world.

The geographic placement was not what I had wanted, my workload was far from ideal, and I was sure that I would never learn most of my students' names; but I was fully engaged and mindful that it was up to me to make this the soul-enriching experience I longed for. And, without a doubt, it definitely turned out to be so.

CHAPTER 8

POODLES, GERMAN SHEPHERDS, AND OTHER DOGS

It's Friday—garbage day. I hate Fridays. But I have to get up. I have to get dressed. I have to eat breakfast. Juan will be coming at 7:50 a.m. to pick me up. I brace myself against the damp air that surrounds me as I lift the heavy blankets away. My body aches from the weight of the blankets; these thick wool covers piled on me every night exhaust me. I pull on my fleece robe and step into alpaca fur-lined slippers. On my way to the bathroom, I peer into the kitchen—the wood-burning stove is dark—not a single ember is visible. I anticipate a cold shower and I am not disappointed. The propane tank is empty again. These frigid showers are barely tolerable. My breakfast is ready—yogurt, banana, slice of bread with cheese, and a cup of instant coffee.

I don't mind the chilly shower or the sameness of every breakfast—except on Friday. I don't want to leave the house on Friday even though Friday is a short work day. I teach only two classes and then walk to the house from school. It's a 30-minute walk I can tolerate—except on Friday. I could take a taxi, but that wouldn't change Friday into Thursday, Wednesday, Tuesday or any other day of the week.

Thank goodness the curtains in my room are still closed. I won't have to look outside. I still have ten minutes before Juan arrives. I don't have to open the front door until then. I can still pretend it's not Friday.

I am in Chile in a small southern town located near *Ruta Nacional 5*, which is part of the Pan-American Highway. (Ironically, U.S. Interstate 5 skirts my hometown.) I am here to teach. Almost every Friday I ask myself, *How did I, a 73-year-old divorced woman, end up at the bottom of the world?* More precisely, at the bottom of the South American continent? The only answer I come up with is that I wanted a change. Change, I had convinced myself, is sometimes necessary in order to move forward. Well, that wasn't clear when I filled out the application forms to teach English to teenagers who, most assuredly, would be oblivious to my quest for change.

Juan, my around-the-corner neighbor and co-worker, pulls up in front. His car headlights are dimmed by the heavy fog that shrouds the town most winter mornings. Shoot— another morning obstacle! And he's late again. His windshield is still cloudy, the defroster hasn't kicked in yet, but I can tell he's already talking, texting, or whatever else he does with that gadget in his hands. How important could anything be that it couldn't wait the ten minutes it takes to get to the high school? I think he has a girlfriend he talks to as soon as he leaves his wife and kids. He normally talks, texts, and reads emails as he drives through town shifting with his right hand, holding the steering wheel with his left texting hand.

Juan, I say repeatedly, *"You are a wonderful driver, you have great eyesight—you saw that biker (pedestrian, dog, car, etc.) before I did, but I would like to get to the US in one piece."*

He always laughs.

Just as I walk back from the high school at the end of the school day, I could also walk there, but that would mean getting up much earlier—and the half-hour walk in the dark winter mornings, carrying my laptop, school supplies, and lunch would be like experiencing a week of five Fridays. I can't do it. So I endure Juan's daily gamble with death.

The señora of the house has unlocked the three security locks of the front door and also the lock on the iron gate of the iron fence that surrounds the entire house. Her children have tried to convince her that so much precaution is not necessary since the Department of Special Police Investigation is headquartered right across the street.

"Yes, but in whose pocket are the police?" she always replies.

She then waits for me to leave so that she can secure every lock again before going back to bed.

I put on my jacket, pick up my bags, and head out the door. Just as I imagined, the street is filled with dogs. Each garbage can is surrounded by two or three dogs trying to topple the can so that they can get to the contents. This may be the only food they get for days.

It seems that the same group of dogs surrounds the same garbage can each week. There are a couple of groups that make me especially sad: the white toy poodle with the gimpy hind leg and the beautiful but emaciated German shepherd, working as a team to tear apart the plastic bags that fill the chosen can; the other group, two shaggy German shepherds and another very thin white poodle circling an overflowing can, trying to pull the contents out. I hope to keep my eyes closed and imagine how they might look if properly fed and groomed—but Juan's cell phone use has me worried as he brakes, shifts, and accelerates our way through town.

Dogs were not a special interest of mine before I arrived in this country. We always had dogs when I was growing up, but those were my mother's dogs. I can't remember requesting any type of pet. When my own children wanted a dog, we purchased a fine purebred black Labrador that I acquired a few years later when they went off to college. Lily lived to be 15. I never thought much about dogs after that.

These are not the only poodles or German shepherds I see. There are many dogs locked behind fences that bark at me as I walk home after my teaching day. But the two breeds—the poodle and the German shepherd—I notice most often. They must be or must have been the preferred breeds in this town—a similar redundancy to the repetitive names of my students.

I was amazed to see such a sea of dogs during my first walk around the capital city after my arrival. There were dogs in groups of three or four or more, dogs in pairs, or alone, roaming the streets, sleeping in the middle of sidewalks and under trees in the parks. I can still recall the look of an elderly dog stumbling along, taking one step at a time, resting and finally collapsing near my table in an outdoor café. His eyes expressed such confusion.

Fridays magnify the dog issue for me. It saddens me to see these forgotten creatures forage through the garbage. During the rest of the week the scene is a little different. The dogs lick the sidewalks when they smell the remains of some dropped morsel; they follow people who have left restaurants or grocery stores hoping to catch some crumb that might fall or be thrown to them; they sit and wag their tails trying to endear themselves to anyone who passes by. Some have staked out a particular territory and wait most of the day in anticipation of receiving a handout from the person who had been kind in the past. There are so many of them—lying in the middle of sidewalks, in the streets, in front of closed doors, and in front of locked gates to houses from which they have been shunned. Some have hollowed out areas beside tree trunks into which they curl during the heat of the day, and again when the cold mist and fog envelope the town.

These street dogs rarely bark. For me their silence and emaciation is profoundly disturbing. When I ask why there isn't something done about this cruelty, the reply most often is that *it used to be worse, or we are used to it, or we don't really notice the dogs.* But how have so many dogs ended up wandering about? My friends explain that people get puppies, they're cute, but then they cost money to feed, and they make a mess in the house, and tear up the yard, and so they are thrown into the street to fend for themselves.

I shouldn't worry, I am told—the dogs are so smart, they even wait on street corners until the traffic lights change.

I cannot bear to look into the eyes of the dogs I encounter on my way home from work. I can't sleep well at night when I have seen some unspeakable depravation during the day. I feel a profound dislike for the people of this town, and sometimes this dislike goes beyond the borders of the town, encompassing all the inhabitants of this country—at least all the citizens of the towns I have visited where I have seen deserted and starving dogs.

I don't want to feel this way. I am sure that this extreme sorrow contributes to my current ill health, but the doctor tells me that I am allergic to the humidity and the mold, not to the sad state of the dogs, and prescribes pills. I think he has misdiagnosed my condition. No point arguing his conclusion, there are only a few more Fridays to come before I leave for home.

By the grace of God, Juan and I arrive in front of the school without incident. Several dogs are waiting as I get out of the vehicle. I open my lunch sack and throw everything but the apple and banana toward them. A small tussle ensues, and then there is a satisfied quiet as each gulps the portion it has won. I plan to buy myself something to eat on the way to my host's house—and hope no dog takes notice as I walk along eating.

There is one little black male dog who lies curled in his hole beside a sycamore tree that I shall remember when I finally leave after completing my volunteer contract with the Chilean Ministry of Education. He lies in the same spot almost every day. He doesn't touch the food I try to give him; he growls at me when I come too close and stands up in a sort of defiance to my attempt to be friendly. His eyes are light brown with a yellowish ring around the iris. He stares at me intently. What is he trying to tell me?

Go home! Feel sorry for some other dog! I'll take care of myself!

And there is the little white and brown spaniel who sits near a bench in the town square waiting for the old woman who comes to feed him occasionally. He takes up his station daily. Should any other dogs approach his chosen spot he barks viciously and chases them away with great fury, using his two front legs, dragging his collapsed hind-end. I wonder what had happened to him—some human cruelty I imagine.

Other dog stories haunt me. Especially the well-intentioned tale of an acquaintance who had tried to rescue two street dogs by taking them home and giving them food and shelter, only to find that their territorial instincts prevailed. They fought continually until one day the stronger of the two killed the other in a vicious confrontation she witnessed helplessly.

One curiosity, aside from the numerous dogs that come and go near the school where I teach, is that there is always a large mongrel dog that sits and watches. As soon as a car approaches he deems is traveling too fast (or so I imagine) he barks and chases after it and tries to bite the tires. He does this repeatedly until the last bell rings and the students have entered the school building. He then leaves, perhaps to guard another chosen site. My hope is that this diligent guardian is being well rewarded for his daily efforts.

As for me, I have accomplished my goal: for a short time, I was a citizen of a community in Chile—not just a tourist in a foreign land.

Now my volunteer service ends soon—only three more Fridays before I leave.

CHAPTER 9

MI FAMILIA CHILENA

Within days of ending my teaching commitment in the Biobío Province of Chile, I was on a bus north to Santiago. The United Airlines flight home, including connecting flights, would take thirty hours. So much time to review and to reflect on the people and places I had hurried to leave.

Very little reflecting, however, occurred. I hadn't realized how exhausted I was until the plane had reached its cruising altitude, and the pilot was welcoming us aboard, assuring a smooth flight ahead, the weather conditions being very favorable. My entire body relaxed, and I promptly fell asleep. I slept most of the trip, only rousing myself when meals were served or to use the restroom.

There never seemed to be a favorable climate to reflect on those extraordinary four months I spent living with the Salvado family while teaching English at the local polytechnic high school. María Elena, the eldest daughter, emails *de vez en cuando* keeping me updated on the family. My responses are always brief and somewhat formal. I have always been reluctant to maintain contact with past friends and acquaintances—a character flaw to be sure in this modern age where constant and prolific communication is the norm.

This year's New Year's greeting, now three years since I lived with the Salvados, sent by María Elena has, however, touched me with its kindness and caring, commanding me to look back and explore that short, but arduous time we shared:

> *Junto a mi madre, deseamos lo mejor de la vida para usted, esperamos haya gozado de una feliz navidad en compañía de sus seres queridos y que pase un muy feliz año nuevo. Se le quiere y anora—muchos cariños.*
>
> *María Elena Torres Salvado*

("Together with my mother, we wish you the best in life, we hope that you enjoyed a happy Christmas in the company of your loved ones and that you will have a happy new year. You are loved and missed—much love.")

The family of Gladys Salvado had been my most intimate contact in Chile. I could have elected to live alone but chose to board with a family. María Elena, Gladys's oldest daughter, would occasionally exclaim, "Señora, you are an angel. There is a reason you are here with us." Perhaps she was right, but even now I have no idea what that reason might have been.

Perhaps I was an angel in that I was an uninvolved witness to a family dynamic that is as old as recorded history: loss, infidelity, discord, blame, and hope for the future.

Gladys Salvado Ortiz was a widow for ten years when I entered her home. Her husband Alfredo had been killed in an industrial accident during his employment at the local, now defunct, sawmill. The company, although not claiming responsibility for the accident, offered to remodel her house by adding a large master bedroom and bath. They also made other improvements to the house; but according to Señora Gladys, they never gave her a monetary settlement. A local attorney advised her to sue for a settlement, but she was adamant about not doing that, saying something about the company having given her husband thirty years of employment at a very good hourly rate of pay. Coming from California where suing is routine without any such consideration, I applauded her reluctance and rationale in her decision not to sue her husband's former employer.

Her widowed older sister Ruth came to live with her and occupied the rear bedroom close to the kitchen. I was offered the second bedroom—the bedroom that Señora Gladys and Alfredo had shared when he was alive—plus the original bathroom and three meals a day.

Señora Gladys and I are the same age; her sister a couple years older. This should by all accounts have been a perfect tenant-and-landlord situation. And for the most part it was. She and I had some wonderful talks around the kitchen table in the late afternoons when her sister was out taking her daily walk or visiting the neighborhood green-grocer's wife. My admiration for her grew as I listened to her story.

She had not been a young bride, at least not by the norms of those times and the place. While waiting and hoping to meet a proper suitor, she enrolled in a cosmetology course offered in a nearby town. Fortunately for her, the local bus conveniently passed almost directly in front of her parents' farm. Señora Gladys never learned to drive although the family eventually bought a car. Upon completion of the course, she and two other cosmetologists stayed in town, rented an apartment, and secured positions in various beauty salons.

It was while working that she met Alfredo, a handsome somewhat older man who would stop and peer into the shop. One day when he had lingered longer than usual, she opened the front door and told him to stop staring at the girls. "*If you want a haircut, you should come in,*" she said—which is what he did.

He would come sporadically, but would always ask for Gladys. One day he admitted (while Gladys was cutting his hair) that he was not getting any younger, that he had a small house, and that he needed a companion. Would Gladys come live with him? Her reply was, of course, she would come live with him, but they would have to stop at the church first and ask the padre to marry them. To her surprise, he said yes. So, with no fanfare, no wedding gown, and no reception, without a single family member present, Gladys found herself committed to a man she hardly knew.

What else was she to do, she asked me in the twilight hours of a cold winter day as we sat in her kitchen warmed by the wood-burning stove. She was approaching thirty, with no other prospects in sight. At least he had a job, a house, and he was good-looking. At the time, she felt lucky that he had chosen her, a woman approaching spinsterhood. She gave up her job and soon two daughters were born: María Elena was first and then Luisa—just one year apart.

She was frugal, a good mother, and what she thought was a loving wife. But Alfredo's "wandering ways" (as Señora Gladys described his repeated affairs) broke her heart. She never confronted him; she never thought of divorce. She settled into a domestic routine denying her own feelings, concentrating on her daughters, and adjusting to her husband's needs. When he was injured at work, she refused the offer of a health worker. He was her husband; he was her obligation. Even now, it makes me sad to think of Señora Gladys's betrayal.

María Elena, her father's favorite (mine also), and Luisa became Señora Gladys's work of art. María Elena, the more academic one, excelled in high school and was allowed to attend the university in a neighboring province. This was made possible when María Elena's aunt, who lived near the university, offered her room and board in exchange for help with domestic chores. When her studies plus the amount of work her aunt expected so overwhelmed her that she became ill, she returned home. Once Alfredo understood the situation, he ordered her to resume her studies. His lovely, smart, and beautiful daughter was not going to be denied a chance to achieve a professional degree. He insisted on paying the aunt for María Elena's room and board with the provision that she was not expected to do any housework. Señora Gladys didn't know how Alfredo managed to pay for this luxury. He never told her and she never asked him.

María Elena did finish her degree and became a licensed School Social Worker for the school district she had attended growing up. She was still working there when I became a boarder in her mother's house.

María Elena is a beautiful woman, not only in appearance but also in demeanor and spirit. Her lovely, oval-shaped face with her large brown eyes and welcoming smile always reminded me of the many depictions of Santa María found in Catholic churches. She is my idealized version of the helpful and kind social worker. Although there is a more than thirty-year age difference between us, we became friends.

María Elena, her husband Pablo Torres, and their three children lived next door to Gladys. In fact, their patios adjoined. The boys, Julio (twelve), Pedro (ten), and Javier (six), were able to go back and forth at will. When their parents' refrigerator didn't have what they wanted, they would run across the patio to investigate their grandmother's supply. Better yet, they would try to find the chocolate Señora Gladys's sister had hidden in her bedroom. Nothing evaded their search when they were hungry, which was all of the time. I remember being hungry like that when I was young;

therefore, I made sure the door to my room was always locked so that my own treats would not disappear.

The Torres family presented a wonderful picture of the ideal young, substantial, hard-working Chilean family trying to make ends meet while paying the cost of a private Catholic school education for the boys and also maintaining a car and a house. Pablo and María Elena had attended the same schools their children now attend. Pablo's family had a higher social status than María Elena's. His father was the manager of the largest sawmill in the province; María Elena's father operated a forklift at the same mill. When the two married, the talk around town was that she was lucky; she had done well for herself. Pablo was a catch.

Perhaps María Elena was a little intimidated by their different backgrounds, but the illusion of his superiority slowly faded as Pablo managed to lose successive jobs, have an affair with their babysitter, and in general shirk his family responsibilities. Their marital difficulties had reached a crisis point just before I arrived. Pablo had lost his current job and was in the process of looking for another. I think it was comforting for María Elena to come and talk with me in the late afternoon at her mother's house. The children were most always at some event, her mother was taking a nap, and the aunt was out on her daily walk and visits. The house was quiet, the kitchen warmed by the woodstove fire, the red wine from the recent grape harvest still mellow.

The place might be different, the circumstances may vary, but the sadness and heartache that come with lost love and disappointment seem to be universal. Last year's email was factual: she and Pablo divorced; the boys were so much bigger now; she moved to a larger house so there would be room for me if I came to visit; her sister Luisa died unexpectedly of an aneurysm just a few weeks prior to her forty-second birthday; their mother was inconsolable.

Yes, Señora Gladys would be inconsolable. Luisa always brought a bit of sunshine and gaiety to her life whenever she came to visit. Luisa was the rebel daughter who threw convention aside and followed her own longings—something Señora Gladys hadn't dared to do but admired, while at the same time shaking her head at her daughter's audacity.

Luisa could hardly wait to finish high school so that she could join her boyfriend Victor, who was studying engineering in Santiago. This was upsetting to both sets of parents: Gladys and Alfredo felt it would be a shameful thing to do without the benefit of marriage; Victor's parents thought he might not finish his studies, and they had hopes of a better match for their handsome and brilliant son. Señora Gladys and Luisa never forgave Victor's mother for not coming to the wedding after their daughter Lila was born.

In spite of his parents' disappointment, Victor did well. He got his degree and was hired by the Santiago Public Works Department as one of their principal engineers. He was hard working and eventually put in charge of some prestigious projects. Luisa was a cheerful and an attractive wife. When their son José was born, she quit her part-time job as a saleswoman in a large department store to take care of their two children and the house. She never asked to have a maid, which would not have been too unreasonable given Victor's position.

Victor saw an opportunity to invest some of his money by buying trucks, which hauled goods from wholesalers to various retail stores. He put Luisa in charge of the scheduling, the hiring of drivers, and so forth. The business did well. They were able to send their children to private schools and buy a home with a swimming pool in a posh Santiago neighborhood.

My respect for the couple grew when, on one of their visits to Gladys, Victor mentioned that he had turned down a university scholarship for his son because he felt that since he could afford to pay the tuition, the university should award the scholarship to a worthy student who, for lack of funds, would otherwise not be able to attend. What an extraordinary generous and spirited act.

Several weeks after that visit, Luisa appeared alone, having driven over 300 miles in a new SUV to her mother's house. She declared that she was leaving Victor and would not return only to be treated like a slave.

"A slave," Señora Gladys intoned.

"Yes, a slave," Luisa repeated.

The new vehicle Luisa had driven from Santiago had brought Luisa's long-standing demand to a head. Neither on the car's title nor on any of the properties they owned was her name attached. She had dedicated twenty years of her life—taking care of their children, the house, and the trucking business—and Victor had not seen it appropriate to acknowledge this. He had given her the new car as a birthday present, but his name was on the title.

"What kind of present is that?" she asked all of us.

Señora Gladys gave her motherly reply. "That's how men are. Don't you love Victor anymore?"

"I don't know. If he loved me, he would've put my name on the title of the car—not his," she shouted at all of us.

"But Lula [using her pet name for Luisa], your father had everything in his name. But now it is all mine."

"I don't want to wait until Victor dies to own a car. Do you know whose fault this is? It's his mother's fault. She tells him what to do and he listens to her. Mama, can I stay here until I decide what to do? All of my clothes are in the car."

Although Señora Gladys didn't want to be pulled into this dispute and the possible rupture of her daughter's marriage, and although she had always liked Victor, her heart went out to her spirited daughter who was so obviously distraught. Yes, she could stay, but what about the young children?

"What young children? They're university students. They can take care of themselves. Besides, they always side with their father. He can take care of them now."

She needed time to figure out how she was going make money. The credit cards and bank accounts were in Victor's name.

Victor would call and ask her to come home. He missed her, and the children missed her. Although he didn't see much of their daughter who had now shacked up with her current boyfriend because she couldn't stand all this tension.

When Luisa did answer his calls, they never seemed to end on a friendly note. Something was happening in Luisa's life. She began to enjoy this freedom. She met up with old classmates and went out with them to the casinos and nightclubs—things that Victor was either too busy or too tired to do.

One Saturday afternoon, Luisa and I were the only ones at home. She announced that she had to take a dress to the dressmaker to have it adjusted since she had lost weight, but she would be back within the hour. Shortly after she left, there was a knock on the front door.

I rushed to open the door thinking that a family member had forgotten their front-door key. There stood Victor. He had left Santiago very early in the morning to make an attempt to talk with Luisa and try to convince her to come home. I mentioned that she had left for the dressmaker and would be home in about an hour. He tried calling her cell phone but no answer. He would visit his mother and try calling her again.

I also tried her number without success. It then occurred to me to call María Elena. She would find a way to contact Luisa. Within thirty minutes, Luisa reappeared and called Victor.

That evening Luisa and Victor arranged to double date with María Elena and Pablo. They would go out to eat and go dancing. Luisa had complained to Victor that they never found time to have fun. Victor, to prove his earnestness to reconcile, agreed. By all accounts, this had been a wonderful evening—but still Victor spent the night at his mother's house and left the next day for Santiago without Luisa.

What I didn't know until much later was that Luisa had connected with a former boyfriend and was trying to weigh her options: stay with Victor or divorce him. Meanwhile, Señora Gladys took the bull by the horns and visited the old boyfriend to make it clear that he was to stay away from her daughter unless he was prepared to marry her. She had no use for such deception. To Luisa she said she was not to bring him home unless they were married—and under no circumstance was she to sleep with this good-for-nothing in her house.

I admired Señora Gladys's gumption. Luisa packed up her clothes and drove back to Santiago—and to Victor, who had promised to put the car in her name.

I'm not sure if Ruth, Señora Gladys's older sister who occupied the third bedroom, ever offered advice or an opinion on Luisa's marital problems or María Elena's issues with her husband. I somehow don't think so. Señora Gladys told me a little about Ruth's life and how she came to live with her. Ruth had been a very smart, attractive, well-dressed career woman when the idea of a woman in Chile having a career was an anomaly. Her job with the Juvenile Correction Division was well paid. She was able to rent an apartment in a good area of Santiago and support herself. Along came an older gentleman, also of independent means, who proposed marriage with only one condition: Ruth was to stop working because no wife of his needed to work since this would imply that he was not capable of supporting her.

Señora Gladys never knew if Ruth gave up her job for love or loneliness, but she did. Señora Gladys, who was by no means a woman's liberation champion, felt sad for her. Her very accomplished sister now found herself in a very controlling marriage. Not only was Ruth too old to have children, lamented Señora Gladys, she soon became a nursemaid to an ailing older husband.

When her husband died, Ruth asked if she could move in with Gladys and Alfredo. Alfredo made it clear that there was no way he would want Ruth in his house. Señora Gladys never explained why Alfredo had such an antipathy toward Ruth. She didn't need to; I understood his attitude. Ruth was simply unpleasant to be around. Within just a couple of weeks after Alfredo's death, Ruth moved in with Señora Gladys.

I am still ashamed of feeling that a burden was lifted from my shoulders as I climbed into the bus and waved goodbye to the Salvado family members who had accompanied me to the bus station. Within a year of my departure, Luisa died, María Elena divorced, Ruth was living with a different sister in another town, and Señora Gladys plunged into a deep depression. Had I been an angel sent to the Salvado family, as María Elena always claimed? But for what purpose? Perhaps my presence gave the family a short reprieve from the inevitable.

CHAPTER 10

CUSTOMS AND HABITS

The Spanish language vocabulary is immense and diverse. In some instances, *modismos*, the colloquial expressions of one region, cannot be directly translated or even understood from one region to another in the same country much less from one Spanish-speaking country to another. Our Spanish language training in the Peace Corps was in the standard or academic Spanish that theoretically can be understood by most, if not all, Spanish speakers around the world. This Spanish served us adequately when reading and speaking Spanish but not so well when trying to understand the very colloquial and idiomatic Spanish we encountered.

The Colombians assert that *hablan el mejor castellano afuera de España* they speak is the best Spanish outside of

Spain. They use castellano to refer to Spanish going back to historical times when the language of Castile, a geopolitical area of Spain, became the official language of Spain. It took me a while to understand that when asked *se toma un tintico* that I was asked if I wanted *café negro*, black coffee. *Tinto* is most always used instead of café. In Colombia, we didn't drink *cervezas*, but *agrias* or *amargas*. *Chicos* and *chicas* are *sardinos* or *sardinas, mi amiga is mi mampa.* By the time I became familiar with a handful of the many, many Colombian colloquialisms, it was time to leave. One singular use of the Spanish *mona* by Colombians will forever be a part of my personal Spanish lexicon.

Shortly after arriving in Bogotà, I decided to stroll down one of the main avenues to become better acquainted with the capital before being assigned to the rural town Sesquilé. I heard someone whistle and call out *mona.* As far as I could remember, *mona* is used when referring to a female monkey. Was someone whistling or calling to his pet monkey? I didn't see a monkey in the vicinity. Strange, I thought. I walked a little further, again a whistle and the word *mona.* And again no sign of a monkey. By the third whistle and a very loud smacking of lips plus *mona,* I knew that this was directed at me. I was aware that much of the Latin world used *gringa* to describe U.S. women. The term then and now is slightly derogatory, but not totally offensive, depending on usage. Was *mona* the word Colombians used for an American woman? Do we look like monkeys or walk like monkeys? I was irritated. Two years of my life was going to be devoted to help Colombian teachers and this is how they would think of me?

When I returned to the Peace Corps office, I asked the bi-lingual Colombian secretary why I was whistled at and why would those men call me *mona?* She laughed a little. "Don't be upset. Colombian men are very forward with their whistles and expressions when the see women on the street they think are attractive. *Mona* is the Colombian word for *rubia*—blond."

"That's a compliment," she added.

It isn't only words that are misunderstood, but also customs and habits. At the end of my second or third full week at a local school, a group of teachers invited me to join them at the restaurant to celebrate the coming Monday. There would be no classes that day, only roundtable discussions about how to incorporate a relatively new teaching concept called "Modern Math" and the 15-minute TV sessions that were based on this into their curriculum.

The restaurant was crowded and the waiters were all rushing around. I was content to chat and wait our turn. My dinner companions had other ideas. Several of them began to snap their fingers or pound the table to attract the waiters' attention. I was mortified. The Colombian Peace Corps secretary, who had become my Colombian guide and resource when in doubt, explained that that was perfectly fine: "How else would the waiter know you wanted to be served?" In the following months, I noticed that many of my fellow Peace Corps members had adopted this practice and were not shy about pounding tables as well and snapping their fingers

There was one custom that none of us, however, fully understood or accepted. We noticed that in the evenings when leaving the house, theater, movie, or other facility, the Colombians would quickly pull out handkerchiefs and cover their noses and mouths We would laugh about it and sometimes mimic walking down the street our noses and mouths covered. My otherwise reliable source, Claudia, had no answer that satisfied my curiosity. According to Claudia, the capillaries in the nose expand in the warm building. Covering the nose and mouth when going out into the cold would allow enough time for the capillaries to adjust and prevent a person from catching a cold. I have not verified this with any U.S. healthcare provider.

On a similar note, when I came home one morning, which was not my usual time to return, I was totally surprised by what I saw. Laid out all around the patio was the family wardrobe. Were they moving without telling me? No. The reason was quite different. The family believed that one shouldn't put on clothes that had been in a cold closet for several days; hence, they laid out the clothes they were going to wear in the patio and let them warm before dressing. This did make sense to me. How much nicer it is to snuggle in a warm bed or put on clothes that have just come from a dryer or fresh clothes that the sun has warmed on a clothesline. Even now, in winter, I put the clothes I am going to wear that day in front of my electric wall heater before getting dressed.

I have no particular religious convictions, but do enjoy going out in our local national forest to choose a perfect fir tree to bring home and decorate for the Christmas holiday. Decorated Christmas trees have become ubiquitous in the western hemisphere In Colombia some fifty years ago, Catholic families, however, preferred to decorate the season with wonderful constructed crèches. My Colombian family used one of the spare tables to set up the most elaborate nativity scene: figurines of the holy family and the Christ child in a manger, as well as the three kings arriving with their presents, the animals that witnessed this most venerated Christian scene. I hope that this is still part of the Christmas celebration in Colombia

My Peace Corps supervisor accused me of going native when I doubted that they were giving the Colombian farmers correct planting advice. Many of the small Colombian farms were situated on the hilly Andean terrain. For millennium the farmers planted their crop in a perpendicular fashion. The agriculture Peace Corps Volunteers were instructed to convince the Colombian farmer that they should plant their crop in a horizontal fashion so that the rain water was caught by the plants and did not run down the mountain unimpeded. I am not sure why I was so convinced that the new methods were wrong. Perhaps I had gone native

Not only were the many colloquial phrases confusing, they, coupled with certain mannerism, pointed out a striking cultural difference. In America when greeting someone, a simple 'Hello, how are you?" suffices. The Colombians are a warm and friendly people. When they encounter someone, they all shake hands while rattling off a string of greetings: *¡Buenos!, ¿Qué hay de nuevo? ¿Qué me cuentas? ¿Qué más?, ¿Todo bien?* All of them used together at each greeting add up to our "Hello, how are you." Although I soon understood this, I maintained the more formal *Buenos días, Buenas tardes, Buenas noches, ¿Cómo está usted?* depending, of course, on the time of day.

Even now, though I can't remember names, faces and interactions are very vivid, and customs that then were laughable I now think endearing. In retrospect, I wish I would have embraced and returned more of the generous and friendly actions that were extended to me.

Part II

CHAPTER 11

THE HORSERADISH CAPITAL OF THE WORLD

My friend George is passionate about horseradish. He has repeatedly explained that not only does horseradish improve the flavor of any meal, it has an abundance of nutritional value, medicinal properties, and—although he is not too sure about this last quality—magical powers to ward off insects and any other unwanted garden or house pests. He is adamant in his defense of this (in my opinion) ugly root vegetable when I dismiss it as just a larger version of the common radish.

He recites the following facts: the medicinal value of both the root and its leaves were known and used as a traditional medicine during the Middle Ages to stimulate the glands, to stave off scurvy, and as a treatment for the common cold.

In fact, horseradish has more vitamin C than most common fruits, including oranges; additionally, it has four times the vitamin C, twenty times the calcium, and three times the iron as any potato. When he still hasn't convinced me to take this miracle vegetable seriously, he enumerates some other amazing facts: rich in thiamine, potassium, magnesium, trace minerals, and proteins, yet desirably low in phosphorous and sodium. And as final evidence of the wondrousness of horseradish, he mentions that his grandmother always planted horseradish around the perimeter of her vegetable gardens to fend off evil spirits.

He hopes to expand his garden by adding horseradish starts which, with care, will provide him with this savory condiment for years to come. Unfortunately, none of the local nurseries carries horseradish starts and no one can tell him where he might find this exotic plant.

"That's odd," I say casually. "You know we live not too far from The Horseradish Capital of the World."

"What?" he shouts. "Why didn't you tell me this before?"

"I didn't know you wanted starter plants for your garden."

"How didn't you know? I've only mentioned how much I like horseradish for the past ten years."

"Liking and growing are two different things. But if you're serious about growing horseradish, let's drive there. It'll be a nice outing—totally different countryside, wildlife preserves, lava beds, and petroglyphs. I haven't been to that area of Siskiyou County for at least twenty years. Are you free to go this Saturday?"

"I'd rather go Friday. Maybe Friday would be better—not so many tourists then.

"George, I don't think there will be many horseradish tourists in that remote corner of California, but Friday's okay by me."

We meet at 10:00 a.m. at my house on the designated day. Before heading out, George thinks it might be prudent to confirm what I remember about Tulelake. Our computer search brings up a web page with the heading *Tulelake— Horseradish Capital of the World.* We learn that sixty percent of the world's horseradish is produced there, much of it going to Japan. In June the town sponsors a horseradish festival. Pictures of horseradish fields with lush green leaves and explanations of the growing cycle of the plant almost bring tears to George's eyes. Yes, this is where he will be able to purchase his longed-for plants

Map Quest directions indicate that it will take approximately 1 hour and 44 minutes to travel the 93.7 miles to the center of Tulelake. Great! We will arrive in time to have lunch in one of the restaurants, and presumably, horseradish will be one of the condiments alongside the ubiquitous ketchup bottle.

I have always liked the high desert landscape of California's eastern Siskiyou County—miles of juniper trees, volcanic outcroppings and the regal presence of Mount Shasta from every direction. I turn off the car's air conditioner, roll down the window to enjoy the dry summer air as the car hums along the almost deserted county road before we connect onto the Volcanic Legacy Scenic Byway All-American Road, also known as State Highway 97.

As we ascend to almost 4,000 feet, I am startled. The lovely wooded scenery I remember from years past has dramatically altered. Instead of tall pine trees framed by greenery and indigo sky, barren, spindly black trunks dot the landscape. Wildfires have ravaged the forests, turning the countryside into a moonscape.

This change is prescient; it saddens me. As we descend into Butte Valley, I sense weariness, a lack of energy emanating from every corner. Even the dust devils roaming the parched, plowed fields seem to have a spent their vigor some time ago. We pass through Dorris, located at the north end of the valley. Never a prosperous-looking town, it has now succumbed not only to poverty but also to time: boarded-up buildings, yellow front lawns, and business signs with faded lettering.

As we leave Dorris and head further east, we again find ourselves traveling alone for miles and miles. We pass a huge wildlife refuge and large planted acreages, but no horseradish fields are evident. At least none with plants that exhibit its distinctive large green leaves. We continue eastward, paying close attention to the fields we pass. We turn onto the Volcanic Legacy Scenic Byway E/West Road that leads to Tulelake and still no horseradish fields. Surely, if Tulelake produces sixty percent of the world's horseradish, as the website advertises, we should, by now, have seen large horseradish fields.

"George, let's turn back. We can take a look at the park with petroglyphs and then head home." George, who slept until we reached Dorris, looks astonished and wonders how I could even think of doing that. Horseradish is the reason for the trip not—petroglyphs. I relent.

We arrive in downtown Tulelake. Cars are parked on both sides of the street but there's not a single person in sight. An eerie silence prevails. And this is the lunch hour on a Friday! My imagination conjures up an Alfred Hitchcock movie set depicting a deserted, wind-swept Western town with dust-covered, abandoned cars and tumbleweeds—something dire has happened here. Its citizens have fallen prey to an unconquerable force and vanished. Although we saw plowed and planted fields, we also saw huge tractors and combines standing deserted in fields—another ominous sign. I again mention turning back. George suggests we take a chance, park the car, and investigate the town on foot.

We pass City Hall and read the handwritten notice: *Monday-Thursday open from 9 a.m. to 5 p.m. except noon to 1 p.m., closed on Friday.* As we walk back to our car, we see a doorway ajar with a sign overhead—*Tulelake Growers' Cooperative.* We walk in slowly. The stillness is frightening.

We are about to turn back when we notice a light at the far end of the hallway. George, the brave, walks toward the light. The young man sitting at a desk barely acknowledges our presence. We ask where we might find a horseradish farm in the area.

"Horseradish?" he is perplexed. He isn't sure since he has only been in this office about two years. He can't really tell us who to ask either.

An employee of the Growers' Cooperative not knowing anything about horseradish. Even George is becoming discouraged.

Next we enter what appears to be a tiny Mexican grocery store. The elderly woman working there doesn't understand what we are looking for and I don't know the Spanish word for *horseradish*. We leave and walk on. At the end of the street is a little park dedicated to U.S. veterans. Some of the flags commemorating the various branches of service have seen better days. There is a charming metal sculpture of two men side by side—one a soldier with his rifle, the other a farmer with a shovel.

We walk on. We see a larger grocery store, look inside and ask the clerk about horseradish. No, they don't carry Tulelake horseradish and she doesn't know where we might find some.

We ask the clerk to recommend the best restaurant in town.

"Well, there's two: one's American and the other's Mexican. Take your pick."

A personal inspection is called for. We head to the American restaurant, two blocks away. We open the front door and peek inside. A youngish-looking woman is standing near a counter. Although there are no other customers, she barely acknowledges us.

A downhearted feeling prevails. I suggest we try the Mexican restaurant. We see three diners, a cook, a waiter, and a menu. We sit down and order the taco specials. George, ever hopeful, asks the waiter, "Where's the closest horseradish farm?"

"I don't know. What is 'hose adish,' señor?"

One of the diners—a solid, healthy-looking young man—overhears our discussion and comes to the aid of the waiter.

"You're looking for a horseradish farm? My family's been farming here for generations. There used to be quite a few fields around here. The water issues for the past twenty years caused those farmers to leave. I think there's one farm left— let me show you on my phone. It's off the main road, maybe Road 101 or 111—just past Captain Jack's Stronghold Restaurant."

As we leave, the young farmer stops us, "Let people know what you've seen here. We used to be a thriving community."

We follow his directions, pass Captain Jack's, but can't find the side-road to the promised horseradish farm.

We drive back to the restaurant, surely someone there will know.

Yes, they know about horseradish since they serve it with their famous prime rib dinners. But, no, they don't know where the farm is and the head cook who would know won't be back for a while.

George asks if they have any roots on hand, and if so, would they sell him one? No, that wouldn't be possible since it is needed for their customers.

Is it possible that the citizens of the area don't know they're living in the Horseradish Capital of the World? Had we misread something on the website? George searches his iPhone. At the very bottom of the webpage he spots a Tulelake address and telephone number for an organic horseradish farm. *How had we missed this?*

Soon the reassuring voice of our GPS guides us onto Road 112 (we had been close).

Eureka! In front of us stretches a field with rows and rows of horseradish plants. We follow the road that parallels the field until we reach the address of the farm. We pull into the driveway. Strange, although there are several cars and trucks in the driveway, no dogs bark, and no one comes out to greet us. Have the inhabitants been whisked away by the same force that is so evident in town?

This will be our last attempt to secure George's plants. We are about to drive off when a curly- haired, elderly man opens the front door and inquires if he can help us. We explain our search for the elusive horseradish plant and wonder if he is the owner of the field we saw. Yes, he owns the field, but is retired now. He leases it to a neighbor.

We ask about Tulelake's designation as the Horseradish Capital of the World as the webpage claims. Somewhat sheepishly, he tells us that when he had the webpage designed and posted more than twenty years ago, all that was true. Many farmers over the years switched to planting onions, potatoes, and other crops in higher demand. The area's water restrictions and drought also contributed to agricultural changes. As we are aware, he never took the webpage down.

He shrugs and says, "Just a little fame, just a little history—why not?"

I am about to say that we drove almost two hours on the strength of that webpage—when I see George shake his head. "Don't," he seems to be saying

The retired horseradish farmer picks up a shovel near the barn and asks us to get into his pick-up. We drive together to the horseradish field. He gets out, digs up two organic horseradish roots and hands them to George who offers to pay.

"Nope," he says. "This is just from one horseradish aficionado to the other."

George is elated. These starts will make his dream of having a never-ending supply of horseradish a reality.

I have not checked if the webpage declaring Tulelake to be the Horseradish Capital of the World has been amended or removed since our visit. It doesn't matter. It was once true—now only one man's dream.

CHAPTER 12

SORRY, I HAVE TO GO NOW

A bearded old man sits or stands at the south-end entrance of the shopping center asking for assistance. He is not alone. His faithful and patient companion is always by his side. On sunny days, the dog sports sunglasses. This attracts attention and possibly more donations. In moments of generosity, I assign the bearded beggar the altruistic role of Salvation Army Bell Ringer minus bell and red pot. Off duty, the two amble along Main Street, the dog without glasses, the owner without the slightly pitiful sign hanging around his neck.

My early morning walking route takes me past the city park. When I am early, I catch a glimpse of a young woman, early twenties perhaps, in her bedroll sleeping under a tree.

Later in the day, I might see her sitting on a bench in front of a closed retail store. She is disheveled and looks a bit disoriented. I wonder why she is willing to while away so much of her youth in this fashion.

Others come to mind. There is the darkly tanned man in a red and sometimes grey T-shirt, jeans, tennis shoes, and backpack who walks with a determined stride around town. I imagine he walks with such purpose to blend in and distract from his aimlessness. When I see him emerging from under the stadium bleachers as I walk around the high school track, I hurry off.

He seems more dangerous than the other men and women shuffling about here and there. He is well proportioned. His clothes and backpack appear to be in good condition. His hair is neatly trimmed, exposing a large bald spot that is as tanned as his arms and neck. I avoid looking into his face. I imagine it is tanned. And although I see him often, I have no recollection of his features. I wish he would disappear. I want him to leave town.

Men and women push shopping carts through town heaped with their belongings flopping about. These carts seem burdensome, requiring many stops. I understand this burden. Although my bundle of possessions is relatively small, it is often burdensome—needing cleaning, repairing, and guarding. Other men and women sport only a sack or backpack. They seem more upright. Maybe they decided early in their lives not to be encumbered by stuff. Maybe they do not need my concern. Maybe they once had homes and possessions, but lost them through unforeseen circumstances and decided that to replace what they once owned was not worth the effort.

I don't want to look at these wanderers, these invaders, but their numbers have grown and it is impossible to ignore their sad and perplexed faces.

I am forced to recognize that this remote Northern California town in which I live no longer is removed from the rejections, failures, and disappointments of modern life, and that my back yard no longer is my haven. These unwelcome invaders surround me.

Several mornings ago, my neighbor approached me to ask if I had heard a scraping noise around midnight coming from the front of my closed garage door. No, I had not heard that particular noise, as the detached garage is at some distance from my bedroom window. She had been sitting on her back porch smoking a last cigarette before retiring when she heard the scraping sound coming from my garage. A six-foot wooden fence divides the length of our properties with the exception of a four-foot stone hedge portion near the location of my garage. She said she crept along the wooden fence and stopped just before the beginning of the stone hedge, hoping she would not become obvious. What she saw amazed and frightened her. A man was raking the cement apron of my garage with a metal rake, over and over again. He was making a semi-circle. Careful not to make a noise or in any way reveal herself for fear of being hit over the head with the rake, she extinguished her cigarette, tiptoed up her back porch steps, slowly opened the screen door, and slid inside. Once in the house, she made sure every door and window was locked.

I had heard a noise that evening, but not a scraping sound, more like a heavy thud. I have not only a two-car garage, but also a carport located more conveniently to the back-door entrance of the house. This is where I keep my garden tools in the summer. The noise was not unusual, as deer and raccoons often prowl around at night. Raccoons are especially prone to chase some unfortunate cat or squirrel into that area and knock things about.

The noise woke me. Had I brought my cat in for the night? I wasn't sure. I got out of bed, put on my robe, went into the kitchen and opened the back door. As I stepped outside, I noticed a man walking slowly away from the carport area. When he saw me, he casually said, "Sorry, but I have to go now."

He had to go now! What had he been doing in my back yard to begin with?

When my neighbor told me what she had seen, I checked the front of my garage. Yes, a semi-circle of rake marks could be seen. How strange was that! Was the man who had so matter-of-factly said, "Sorry, but I have to go now" the same man who had made the semi-circles? Had he imagined some unfinished chore in another place, another time?

These invasions into my space are not new, they have been ongoing.

One cold September evening, I heard a desperate knock on my front door. Living alone, I am uncomfortable opening the door late at night, but the woman's voice pleading with me for help worried me. I opened the door to a distraught looking young women standing on the porch.

"Please, can I use your phone? My four-year-old is missing. I fell asleep and when I woke up I couldn't find her. I live next door. I locked myself out. I don't have my phone. I need to call my mother. Maybe she has my daughter."

I confess, I am not acquainted with the tenants in the "Victorian lady"—as I refer to the apartment house next door. The tenancies are short. I only know there is a new tenant when there is a change in cars parked in front. Against my better judgement, I let her in. She used my cell phone to call her mother, but couldn't contact her. I advised her to call 911.

Less than ten minutes later two squad cars pulled up. Tall and imposing in their riot gear, the officers entered the foyer of the apartment house. For lack of a key, they broke down the hysterical young woman's apartment door and entered. Surprise! But I believe I was the only one surprised; the daughter was asleep in her bed.

I never saw the young woman or child again.

What had confused the young woman? Had she imagined herself or her daughter to be somewhere else after waking from a possible drug-induced sleep?

I feel disheartened: my life has grown more restricted. My little 1945 cottage, nestled between two historic houses on a quiet tree-lined street, no longer embodies my dream of a safe haven. I can no longer leave my doors or windows open to catch the breezes on warm summer nights. I have modified my daily walks. I no longer feel safe walking alone on country roads or in the park. I have been advised to be more cautious in all my movements and, if possible, acquire a gun—something I have never contemplated and refuse to do. I feel more inhibited when encountering people I do not know. I do not greet them with a smile nor look them in the eyes.

I would like to tell all the strangers who have invaded my life and changed my reality, "Sorry, but you have to go now."

CHAPTER 13

MY HISTORIC STREET

I live in a historic town, on a historic street, between two historic houses. To my immediate east is the C.C. Cady House built in 1902. My first impression of the house was that it resembles a boat in dry-dock. The jutting front porch is the bow of the vessel. Its long frame ends with a back porch that has the appearance of a rudder attached to the stern. The house looks strong and secure, giving the impression of having weathered many storms.

My historic neighbor to the west is the 1899 R.S. Taylor House. I think of it as a forgotten Victorian lady. I would like to have met her when she was young and stately, receiving attention and admiration from the local gentry. Her appearance now is worrisome. Abuse and neglect have diminished her beauty. Her filigree has been ripped and torn, water stains and patches are evident on her bodice, and bald spots are more numerous each year in her once lovely crown. I imagine the moaning sounds coming from the tall cedar trees that separate our properties when the winds blow on cold autumn nights, to be the lady's soft cries for help. Those who once cared for her and loved her are no longer present.

Further down the street are other homes that have had more fortunate histories. The Methodist Parsonage built in 1889, now a two-story apartment building, has most recently received a new soft gold-yellow coat. It now shines like I imagine the first gold nugget shone when it was pulled from the ground at Discovery Park in Yreka in 1851. Beautiful gardens filled with roses, daisies, lilies, flowering trees, and green lawns are part of the 1905 Jesse Davis House. A handsome wrought-iron fence surrounds the house and grounds. It is obvious that its current owners appreciate and cherish the essence of their property. St. Mark's Episcopal Church, built in 1880, now part of the Yreka Preservation Corporation, is an outstanding example of enduring historical and architectural simplicity and elegance.

I have mentioned only a few of the homes at the lower end of Lane Street honored with plaques stating the name of the original owner and date of construction; there are many others that add to my street's history and character. As Lane Street continues west, newer and more modern houses line the street. At the most western end, however, history asserts itself again. A cattle guard and sign, advising that the street is now *a country lane, private and restricted,* has been posted. This was not always the case. I remember a historical marker there not so many years ago, stating that the street and lane were once part of *California/Oregon Stage Road from 1851 to 1886.* Although the sign has been removed, either by design or vandalism, I hope that the essence of the site, as well as the character of the homes—past, present, and future—will awaken in those who reside here the gentle historic ambience of Lane Street.

CHAPTER 14

A SNOWY WINTER DAY

It had snowed during the night and most of the morning. I sensed the snow as soon as I woke up—there is a deep silence when snow first blankets our town. Gradually, the day began—the morning light illuminated a lovely winter scene—at times tiny flakes presented themselves as a soft curtain quietly raining down on the landscape, at other times huge flakes floated like feathers from the sky. In Germany, children are told that it snows when *Mutter Hulda* in the heavens is shaking out her feather pillows and comforters. I like this image. It brings back good feelings I have about my childhood in my grandmother's house in a small town in the foothills of the Bavarian Alps.

My cousins and I stayed with Oma during the hard times after World War II while our parents tried to reconstruct their lives and earn a living. Winter was especially wonderful there. My cousins and I would snuggle together in the huge beds covered with down comforters and pillows and then wake up to the frosted windows. The cook stove provided the only heat, but it didn't seem to matter. The kitchen was always warm since Oma had gotten up hours before. Breakfast was readied as we dressed. So many years later, I can still taste the hot *Ersatz Kaffee* with powder milk into which we dunked our thick slices of *Schwarzbrot*, black bread. I loved the taste of the powder milk even without the imitation coffee that Oma received each month from the German government as the widow of a World War I veteran.

I have a wonderful view of the street from my home office window. I watched as the snow transformed the neighborhood—the lawns became white carpets, the roofs, blanketed a downy white, and the trees and bushes decorated with a post-Christmas elegance. I watched as a neighbor shoveled his walkway and sidewalk. Perhaps he had listened to a weather report that predicted more snow. Perhaps he hoped that the current shoveling would make the task easier when the anticipated snow arrived. I have done this in the past, but had no wish to disturb the gorgeous snowfall—time enough to tackle the task if the snow and ice haven't melted in a few days.

As the day progressed, I occasionally glanced at my neighbor's bare sidewalk and steps leading to the front door. A tiny spark of guilt! I admitted the neighbor is more civic minded. I saw the mailman deliver the neighbor's mail with ease. I began to worry he might slip and hurt himself attempting to deliver mine. I put on my winter boots, heavy jacket and mittens, and headed out to retrieve the snow shovel from the garage.

It was great to be outside. I started with the front steps then moved onto the short walkway. The snow was light, not yet compacted or iced over. Foot traffic had hardened the snow on the sidewalk, making the work a little more difficult, but not impossible.

Humming along, shoveling the snow this way and that way, I was mindful of the town's snow removal rules not to clear the snow onto the street which would cause the drains to overflow. Satisfied that I was not in gross violation of the snow removal mandate, I stopped to appraise how much further I needed to shovel to reach the end of my portion of the sidewalk. Looking up, I saw a young man standing a few feet in front of me. I had not seen or heard him approach. In fact, I had not seen or heard anyone walking along my street the entire time I was outside. Where had he come from? He didn't look like someone from town—a handsome young man in his twenties, dressed as though he had just stepped from the pages of an upscale sport's magazine, wearing the current approved apparel for men. His gaze was disconcertingly direct when he asked if he could finish shoveling the sidewalk and my driveway. (My first thought: had I even combed my hair that day?) I told him that I was almost finished with the sidewalk and was not going to tackle the snow in the driveway. My Jeep was capable of getting me out if necessary. He wanted to know if I was sure, he was very happy to help. His beautiful eyes, so clear and bright gave me a questioning look, "Was I sure?" Yes, I was sure. I don't know why I was so uncomfortable. I told him he was kind to offer his help but that shoveling snow was a good form of exercise, it was good for me. I looked down, somewhat embarrassed not to have accepted his help. An eighty-year-old woman shouldn't mind accepting help! When I looked up, he was gone. How had he vanished so quickly? I stepped into the street to get a better view, but no one was in sight.

This interaction still puzzles me. I have had similar experiences: being helped by two strangers who magically appeared to carry me across a huge mudslide in the Andes and then just as magically disappear; a solitary vehicle appearing suddenly on a deserted street in time to collide with an enormous dog as it was leaping in anger toward me; a busy freeway becoming impossibly vacant as my car careened across several lanes after hitting an oil slick, and others. How to explain these occurrences? Was it luck or was it an extraterrestrial force coming to my rescue? Perhaps luck is that extraterrestrial force, that interceding energy, we are all blessed with from time to time.

It snowed again, as predicted, the following day. I decided to let nature take charge of my sidewalk and walkway, and it did. By the end of the day it rained, clearing away the snow and creating a small river flowing toward its destiny, the drain.

CHAPTER 15

EARLIEST MEMORY AND CHICKENS

I'm not sure how to separate my personal childhood memories from my mother's stories. My mother was a storyteller supreme. At almost every evening meal, she would elaborate on some event she had experienced during her workday. But often a memory of her past would be our entertainment. No one dared to interrupt to remind her that we had heard this or that story before. I think we could all tell the same stories. We knew that Uncle Georg was so good looking that all the girls were after him, but he disappointed the whole family by marrying the ugliest one. Or that Aunt Anna would threaten to throw herself in the local pond if she had to memorize one more Bible verse for the weekly religion class. The characters in my mother's life are still very present in my own.

The one story she would tell me repeatedly when I was very young was when we had chicken for dinner. I remember it so vividly that I am going to claim it as my earliest childhood memory. We lived in an upstairs apartment in a large farmhouse. The family across the hall from us had a son, Hans, who was my age. Downstairs was occupied by the landlady, Frau Pullman. A stream flowed through the field behind the house. Both mothers would remind us daily not to go near the creek when they sent us outside to play. Our punishment would be severe if they caught us even close to the water. At a very young age, I knew it would mean a spanking for me. I also knew that Hans's mother would scream at him from her upstairs bedroom window when he was a bad boy. She was an invalid and didn't often leave her room.

Hans and I must have gotten bored one day and dared each other to go down to the creek. By some unfortunate timing (mother would always say "fortunate"), she had come down to look for us. When she didn't see me, she went down to the creek, and of course, there we were. Not one to be shy about following through on pronouncements, she spanked me. She took Hans by the hand and led him back to the yard.

Frau Pullman, my good friend, who had witnessed the spanking, told mother that she should rest and not stress herself so much (mother was pregnant with my sister)—she would watch me. Frau Pullman took me by the hand and led me to the small shed where she kept the chicken feed. She helped me fill a small container. We then walked back to the chickens roaming free in the yard. Frau Pullman knew I loved to feed the chickens. She also knew that this distraction helped me forget the punishment. I truly loved those chickens and Frau Pullman. To this day, I refuse to eat chicken meat.

Ursula Bendix was born in Germany in 1945 and immigrated to Portland, Oregon, with her family to when she was ten. After receiving her undergraduate degree from Portland State University, she joined the Peace Corps as an Educational Television Volunteer in Colombia, South America.

At the end of her two-year volunteer service, she returned to Portland, completed her master's degree, and finished working on a secondary school teaching credential. She moved to Yreka, California, in 1976 and taught adult education and Spanish at College of the Siskiyous. She also taught at a polytechnic high school in southern Chile in 2018 as part of the English Open Doors program sponsored by Chile's Ministry of Education and the United Nations.

This is her second book of stories. The first are stories centered in Siskiyou County: *Land · Home · Mountain View*.